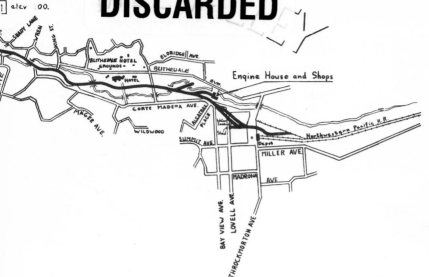

Mt Tamalpais
&
Muir Woods
Railway

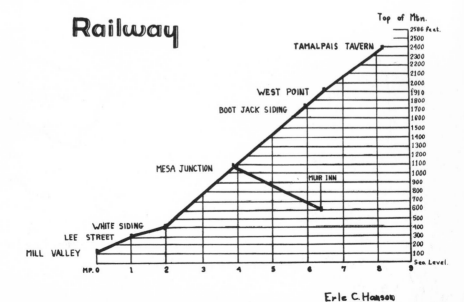

Erle C. Hanson

6-2-61

THE CROOKEDEST RAILROAD
IN THE WORLD

AT THE SUMMIT OF TAMALPAIS

Mountain locomotive No. 5 prepares for the eight-mile return trip to Mill Valley. Tip of the half-mile high Marin County peak appears at upper left.

THE
CROOKEDEST RAILROAD
IN THE WORLD

*a history of the Mt. Tamalpais
and Muir Woods Railroad
of California*

•

by Theodore G.
WURM

and Alvin C.
GRAVES

Berkeley • HOWELL-NORTH • California
1960

Published by Howell-North Books

1050 Parker Street, Berkeley 10, California

FOREWORD

We who lived through the entire era of the Mt. Tamalpais Railroad will, with keen interest and a thrill, go back through that period while reading and reliving the story of the most romantic of mountain railways. Californians of the later generations and railroad lovers throughout the world will find in this history of a great project a tale of railroad construction, success, competition, and failure.

Most of us who were neighbors of the road still remember the dust of grading and the dull distant boom of blasting when it was being built, and the gangs of men coming and going through Mill Valley while working on the construction. It was quite an experience, and one long remembered, for us small boys to go down to the depot and watch little wood-burning "498," the first locomotive. The road was only a few weeks in operation when my whole family made the trip to the top of Tamalpais by train. As a result of the twisting and turning and the rapid rise in elevation, one little Graves boy was very sick upon arrival, and I recall the family returning to the valley on the same train.

Ten years later all memory of sickness was put aside and I was the happiest young man in town, when, for several months, I was a fireman on the quaint locomotives. The large crowds on Sundays and holidays are recalled, the two and three extra trains to take them to the top, the thrill we got in the engine when we rounded Horseshoe Curve at the head of Blithedale Canyon and the passengers could get a good look at the laboring engine, with cranks and shafts turning, and the roar from the smokestack pushing a column of smoke skyward. We and the engine then became, as our Superintendent Mr. Thomas would say, "a part of the scenery."

The thrill of being admired was short lived, however, for within a few rods uphill from the curve the marvelous panorama of the entire bay and cities would burst into view and all the crowd would rise up as a unit in rapture at the scene below them. Further thrills came at the curving and twisting route up the mountain and through the "Double Bow-Knot," the stops to take on water for the thirsty locomotive, the pause at West Point to disembark passengers for the Bolinas Stage and to deliver the mail, and the final grand entree through the arch at the "Tavern of Tamalpais" and the unloading of the passengers.

Memories arise of the extra fine meals the train crew would have in the kitchen at the Tavern, and the genial chef, Willie Lee, who always invited us to get anything we liked out of the ice box; our stay overnight when it was storming, listening to the wind howl around the eaves of our dormitory; the sway of the engine and cars when the strong winds would catch us on the ridge along the top of the mountain between East and West Peaks. It was a great day for engineer Jake Johnson and me when we were given the honor of taking the first passenger train into Muir Woods. Two cars crowded with school children from Mill Valley were taken up, and many stops were made to let the kids take in the view and sing songs. It was a happy day for them and for the train crew.

Who of the old-timers in Mill Valley does not recall the little Blithedale Dinkey, the local train that ran up the canyon to Lee Street and back with shoppers and commuters? And Cliff (Hank) Graves, the father of co-author Al Graves, who was conductor of the local at the advanced age of fifteen years? And Bonner Whitcomb and Joe Marshall as engineers on little Engine No. 6?

Time rolled on; the automobile came on the scene; the public took to it. Result: an auto highway to the top of the mountain. So, as with many other railroads, the little Tamalpais mountain line was caught in the tide and had to bow with its many brothers and sisters to the march of progress. Now, through the work of many hours of research and months of collecting data and stories and pictures, those days of the "Crookedest Railroad in the World" are lived again in this book. I know that authors Ted Wurm and Al Graves, who have been interested in railroad history and operation since their youth, have given us an excellent story of the railroad.

ROY D. GRAVES

San Francisco, California
1954

ACKNOWLEDGMENTS

The authors wish to acknowledge their gratitude to the following persons for assistance in the preparation of this history of the Mt. Tamalpais & Muir Woods Railway:

Roy D. Graves, Richard E. Meyer, Jasper Walk, Paul Darrell, Grahame Hardy, the late Randall V. Mills, Rev. John McGloin, S.J., Jeanette Hitchcock and the Hopkins Transportation Library at Stanford University, Robert Hanft, Brian Thompson, Lawrence O'Hare, Frederic Shaw, Wallace Sorel, William Pennington, Douglas Richter, Volley Thoney, Miss Ann Fisher, Albert Cunningham, W. E. Waste, C. A. Graves, Erle C. Hanson, and Mrs. James Jenkins, daughter of the railroad's president.

TO THE MEMORY OF

HENRY CLIFTON (HANK) GRAVES
*who began his extensive railroad
career on the Tamalpais Line.
Of all the "pikes" he served on,
he loved this one best.*

CHAPTER ONE

PLANNING and CONSTRUCTION

Corporation Formed . . . The Railroad is Started . . . The
First Engine . . . McInnes and His Gun . . . The First Train

North across the bay from San Francisco, in the very heart of "marvelous" Marin County, rises impressive Mount Tamalpais. From its tip, 2600 feet above the bay, one views almost a third of California; and from great sections of central California, in return, a person looking westward can see the "sleeping maiden" outline of friendly Tamalpais rising like a silhouette at the very ocean's edge.

The mountain got its unusual name from the Miwok Indian *tam'-mal* (bay country) and *pi'-is* (mountain). Right up to the present day it has been to the city folk around the bay almost what Fujiyama is to the people of Japan, an object of devotion. It has held in their affections the place of an ever-ready comrade with whom to spend a happy holiday. Beloved alike by the hardy hobnailed hiker and the sophisticated, it is dedicated democratically to the Sunday Picnicker, the painter and the poet, and the dramatist. An annual event attracting thousands is the play staged in an open-air glade by the Mountain Play Association.

For more than half a century tramping in the Tamalpais country has been very popular with San Franciscans. It was the traditional Sunday outing to "catch" the ferry at the foot of Market Street, then the connecting narrow-gauge train from Sausalito into a wooded valley at the mountain's eastern base and the town of Mill Valley. Scores of excellent trails were extended over and around the mountain, reaching into every glade and glen, seeking out the spots of panoramic beauty and the quiet hideouts of cottontail and deer.

In the beginning, as again in the last thirty years, it was necessary for the sightseeing hiker to tramp all the way to Tamalpais' half-mile-high summit by one of the rugged trails. But during the thirty-year interval at the start of this century, when the "Mountain Railroad" was operating it became the accepted custom to ride the train to the summit and hike down. And millions of ordinary travelers and tourists were able to grasp the pleasure of this grandest of mountain trips without laying a foot to the trail; they rode the Tamalpais Railway steam train to the top, coasted by gravity car down into lovely Muir Woods, and took the steam train back into Mill Valley for the "greatest day's outing in the World."

It is naturally fitting that this county of Marin derived its name from a famous chief of the Lacatuit Indians, who frequented the southern part of the peninsula. The Indian people held Tamalpais in superstitious fear, feeling that the top of the mountain was inhabited by evil spirits. Between the years 1815 and 1824 Chief Marin, aided by his people, is said to have vanquished the Spaniards in several skirmishes for supremacy.

But so beautiful a spot as Marin County was destined to attract the settlers who flocked to California after its discovery of gold. Ferry service to San Francisco was started in the 'Fifties, carrying commuters from old Sausalito and the regions adjacent to Tamalpais. Mill Valley, headquarters of the Tamalpais mountain railway, got its start as Eastland, the first streets being surveyed and laid out in 1889. The town became Mill Valley on September 1, 1900, and it has been pointed out as a California beauty spot ever since.

Across the southwestern face of Tamalpais, lying in a deep, peaceful canyon between the mountain and the sea, is world-famous Muir Woods, set aside as a United States Monument in 1908. This sylvan wilderness was named in honor of John Muir (1838-1914), the celebrated California naturalist. There are about 425 acres in the park and more than three-fourths of the trees are towering mammoth redwoods thousands of years old. Their massive trunks reach 200 to 300 feet into the air. The trip through this forest is a delight, the roadway following a mountain stream, Redwood Creek. Paths are thickly carpeted with redwood bark and fallen leaves; the banks are masses of ferns, and the soft air is filled with aromatic fragrances of the woods.

All of this beauty lies within an hour's ride of San Francisco, over the Golden Gate Bridge and to the summit of Mount Tamalpais by good paved highway. Only a few years ago the trip took twice the time by ferry and the "Crookedest Railroad in the World"; yet it was many times more picturesque and interesting. This was through the agency of the Mt. Tamalpais and Muir

Woods Railway, begun in a flare of excitement and grand plans — even in an appropriate amount of the champagne so dear to the inaugural celebrations of the Virginia and Truckee and other glamorous western short lines. Born in 1896, the railroad was destined to serve with the faithfulness of a trolley line for some 34 years, through fat periods and lean, finally to die forgotten in 1930.

The Mount Tamalpais railroad drew people from all over the United States and from many foreign countries to Marin County. Every travel guide mentioned the crooked railroad and its wonderful engineering, and the thrilling trip up and down the mountain. Every national tour party included Mount Tamalpais in its itinerary, often filling guidebooks with lengthy descriptions of the wonders of the region and playing up in admiration the excellent construction and operating methods of the railway. Every famous person who visited San Francisco during more than a score of years crossed over the bay to Marin and Tamalpais, was carried in awe and wonder to the Summit to be wined and dined at the tavern. The people of the Bay Area considered it an obligation to take important guests up their mountain; every world traveler knew and spoke in glowing terms of the trip to the summit of Tamalpais by rail.

Progress has come and has erased the Tamalpais railroad from existence. But the route of the railroad still serves as an important fire trail; there are other relics here and there — a water tank or two, the platform at the site of Mesa Station (the famous "Double Bow-Knot"). And the "Mountain Road" will live forever in the hearts of Marin County people, particularly those of Mill Valley, who came to look upon their railroad as a faithful friend, always handy but seldom noticed, until the day arrived that it suddenly disappeared. From that moment, as is always the case, it has been missed and its passing has been deeply regretted.

Incorporated in January, 1896, as the Mill Valley & Mt. Tamalpais Scenic Railway, the company held its first directors' meeting at 508 California St., San Francisco, on February first, at which time officers were elected, plans were made for financing, construction and operation. President was Sidney B. Cushing, to whom the original idea had been presented by Louis L. Janes of the Tamalpais Land & Water Co. (Mr. Janes was destined to be the railroad's secretary for many years.) Cushing, president also of the San Rafael Gas & Electric Co., had immediately seen the wisdom in Janes' proposal, especially since the construction of such a railroad would undoubtedly bring new business to his Blithedale Hotel summer resort, up Corte Madera Canyon from the town of Mill Valley. This hotel had been the reincarnation of the sanitarium established in 1879 by Cushing's mother upon the death of his father. It was an ideal locale for quiet, restful vacations.

First financial assistance came from A. E. Kent, father of the late congressman William Kent, who subscribed for $10,000 in stock and gave the right-of-way through his land in upper Corte Madera Canyon.

The practicability of running a railroad up the slopes of Tamalpais without use of cogs or other expensive machinery was demonstrated by Augustus D. Avery, a young surveyor in the employ of the Tamalpais Land & Water Co. Mr. Avery, in charge of the company's survey corps, was instructed to find an easy route. After a number of weeks on the mountain, he announced that a way had been surveyed in such a manner that at no point would there be a grade of more than seven percent.

Undoubtedly Cushing and Janes had a hand in laying out the line as well. In relating the history of the railroad, in 1925, Janes told how he and Sidney Cushing had determined the feasibility of the mountain railroad by running a line with an ordinary hand level and their eyesight. At any rate, a route was laid out that would be relatively easy to build and operate. So a contract was awarded to the California Construction Co. under which they would complete the railroad from Mill Valley to the summit of Tamalpais "in consideration of their subscription for 200 shares of the stock . . ." as stated in the company Minutes. The construction company was to be paid its actual costs, plus 12½% for profit.

Construction was started Wednesday, February 5, 1896, and the plans were extensive indeed. The Mill Valley & Mt. Tamalpais Scenic Railway was to be an electric trolley line, with the power house in Mill Valley. It was to be continued over the top of Tamalpais to Bolinas Beach, on the shores of the Pacific, at that time one of the finest beaches on the coast and virtually inaccessible. Bolinas residents were very interested in having the electric line extended, and the cost would be in the neighborhood of only $100,000, as against an estimate over the million mark for a steam rail line. The San Francisco, Tamalpais & Bolinas Railroad of 1889

The town of Mill Valley, California, looked like this when the Mill Valley and Mt. Tamalpais Scenic Railway was proposed in 1896. This view of the "Plaza" shows depot of the narrow-gauge North Pacific Coast Ry., looking southeast toward San Francisco.

Dear Sir

Sau 30 1896

The first meeting of The Board of Directors of the Mill Valley and Mr. Tamalpais Scenic Railway will be held in the office of Edward G. Stetson 508 California St 3rd floor on Saturday Feb 1st 1896 at 2. o'clock P. m.

Very Truly

Lonro L. James

had barely reached Mill Valley, then been sold to the North Pacific Coast as a narrow-gauge branch line. But this new plan of 1896 sounded more practical. "Bolinas will be a great resort," heralded a local newspaper.

"Work Commenced Last Wednesday Morning" announced the *Eastland Press* for February 8, 1896. "The contracts for engines, boilers, dynamos, wires and other requisites for generating power will soon be let . . . The power house will be situated on the Cushing property (and) will be commenced in a short time." Every train on the North Pacific Coast Railroad brought in a number of prospective laborers, all of them crowding into a jumble of rude shanties just opposite the station.

By February 23rd two hundred men were hard at work, a small force cutting brush from the right-of-way and starting to grade at the Mill Valley end of the line, while another party was stationed on the ridge near the summit to prepare the upper five miles. At the higher camp teams and scrapers had to be supplanted with pick and shovel labor because of the narrow, ten-foot-wide roadbed and the rocky nature of the ground.

The line was to go up Corte Madera Canyon in a north-westerly direction, bridging the creek four times in the first mile, then turning and coming back around the southern face of the mountain. Here it would cross the ridge and, making another turn to the north, stop a few hundred yards short of the actual tip of the mountain peak. Engines and boilers, motors and other electrical fittings had been contracted for. "Capitalists" had, according to one San Francisco newspaper, made offers to build a hotel or resort at the upper terminal, and the North Pacific Coast had promised a new depot at Mill Valley, to accommodate electric trains of the mountain road at one side and their own narrow-gauge steam trains at the other.

Right at the beginning there was trouble involving the men at work on the roadbed high up on the mountain. Numerous laborers had left their jobs by the 26th of February because of overwork and poor food, alleged the *San Francisco Call*, February 27, 1896. The general public was full of sympathy for the workers, who were being paid $1.75 a day for ten hours work, while forced to pay out of this $5.25 a week for board and extra for Sunday meals. All their purchases had to be made at the company store and, the paper reported, most of the men had no more than a dollar left at the end of a week. One of the workers described to

—WILLIAM A. PENNINGTON

MIGHTY TAMALPAIS TO THE NORTH OF SAN FRANCISCO

Mt. Tamalpais, the "Sleeping Maiden," lies guarding the Golden Gate in this 1934 view from over the heart of the city. For generations the mountain has provided rest and relaxation to the people of the area, and it was for 34 years the location of the "Crookedest Railroad in the World."

Sausalito from the ferry was a pleasant sight for sightseers and commuters for nearly a century. This was the way to get to Tamalpais and its crookedest railroad, as shown in the map below, reprinted from an old company travel folder.

—GRAHAME HARDY

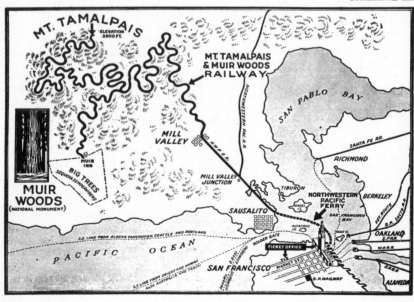

The first locomotive, No. 498, was a Shay-type geared engine, with cylinders on the right side. Above, No. 498 stands beside the first depot in Mill Valley; extra rail in the roadway was for cars of the connecting narrow-gauge. Below, No. 498 with the line's first passenger car No. 5, a converted San Francisco cable, at Fern Canyon tank.

a reporter how they had to get out of bed at five and walk two miles to work after breakfast; then they were allowed one hour for the four-mile march to lunch and back, including time consumed eating "stuff that is vile." When the workmen complained to the company, they were told there were plenty ready and willing to take their places.

It is really not surprising that the people of Mill Valley and the surrounding area were wholly in sympathy with the men. That the public had no love for the railroad people and the construction company is demonstrated by an incident recorded in the local newspaper. The volunteer fire department in Mill Valley owned a large iron triangle, which hung over the entrance of their hall and had been used to give the alarm in case of fire in years gone by. One of the timekeepers for the railroad builder, knowing that the triangle was not in use, carted it away to call the men to supper at the camp.

An infuriated citizen spotted this unfortunate timekeeper in the course of his crime and immediately informed the chief of the fire department. This precipitated a council of war at the firehouse. Finally, a warrant was sworn out for the man's arrest on a petty larceny charge. Deputy Constable E. E. Gray took his search warrant, scoured the camp and found the triangle. Both the culprit and the triangle were brought before Justice of the Peace Tom Fottrell, who imposed a stiff fine, a stern warning, and allowed the representative of the unpopular construction company to depart.

Within a few weeks after the start of grading, great excitement gripped the residents of Mill Valley. "First Engine Has Arrived — The Mountain Road Will Soon Be in Operation" bannered the *Eastland Press* on March 7th, 1896. "Last Wednesday (March 4th) marked an important day in the history of the Mill Valley & Mt. Tamalpais Scenic Railway" continued the story, and almost the entire population turned out for the great event. They watched the husky, standard-gauge locomotive transferred from a narrow-gauge N.P.C. flatcar to an improvised track near the depot. All the leading citizens were there — Lovell White of the Land & Water Co., Michael O'Shaughnessy, civil engineer, Charles F. Runyan, stockholder, George Marsh, Maurice Windmiller, and most likely the Thompson children, one of whom, Kathleen, was later to win a novelist's fame as Kathleen Norris.

The steam locomotive that all turned out to view was a twenty-ton Shay-geared locomotive, loaned by the Dollar Lumber Company from their Russian River logging operations. This fine piece of equipment had been on display at the great Chicago Exposition of '93 and was numbered 498, its construction number at the Lima Locomotive Works in Ohio. The engine came in charge of Jake Johnson, Captain Dollar's first and finest engineer. Jake was scheduled to return to Dollar with his engine in May, but he stayed on to run the first train, then continued with the Mount Tamalpais railroad for 34 years, operating the very last train in 1930. It seems that Jake figured old Captain Dollar was extending himself too far and was sure to go broke, though the old man tried again and again to get Jake back from the Tamalpais line.

Thrilling day, indeed, when the first engine arrived! People wondered about the trolley plans, but the papers were quick to point out that these were still very much in force and that two seventy-passenger electric cars were to be operated, with the Shay engine as a standby in case of larger crowds. President Cushing had been authorized by the directors to purchase a 25-ton Shay for the road, as its own initial locomotive. But Mr. Cushing observed that "the Shay locomotive now used in construction has been found to have some bad features inasmuch as it was prone to jump the track sometimes without apparent cause." The president believed a thirty-ton Heisler-geared locomotive would prove superior and was given permission to arrange for one to be built by the Stearns Manufacturing Co. of Erie, Pa., for the sum of $6425. It would be able to travel 12 miles per hour — not speedy, but with power enough to haul three or four crowded cars up the seven percent grade of the mountain road.

A shipment of crossties arrived at the same time as the engine, and rails a week or two later. Food for laborers had been improved so that, despite hardships from the cold weather, there now was little complaining. A few cases were stirred up by the newspapers as part of their constant heckling campaign against the construction people. One story told of a foreman who, upon resigning, was offered a "balance" of four dollars after nineteen days' work. The company had deducted ten percent of his salary because he quit before the month was up; then they had added ten percent to the price of everything he had bought from the company store during his employment.

On March 7th the teamsters walked off the job when they were told they would have to buy from the company a tin dinner-pail costing 35 cents, and that hot lunches would no longer be available. It seems strange today to read of a company working on a cost-plus basis that would so attempt to cut costs to the bone. Even stranger, a few days later we find the laborers working like demons in an unusual *esprit de corps* when the company met with construction obstacles.

The Tamalpais road seemed destined for trouble, for now a complete blockade threatened the work, titled by the newspapers "McInnes and His Gun." J. H. McInnes was a property owner in the lovely canyon up from Mill Valley depot, one of the wealthiest men of the valley and an individual of great determination. The construction gangs had graded the roadbed about three-quarters of a mile out from the station, and on the 17th of March began laying rails. It developed that the line of the railroad was planned to run for about three hundred yards in Corte Madera Avenue and, in laying out the route along this boulevard, the company thought it best to run the track upon one side of the road. Thus, the rails would come within two feet of the sidewalk in front of McInnes' property, necessitating removal of a fine, large tree.

Several smaller trees had already been cleared and the men were about to tackle this landmark, when the owner appeared on the scene with a six-shooter and stopped the work by threats to kill the men who were carrying it out. Discretion being the better part of valor, and their pay being what it was, the men fled to a safe distance and left the field to McInnes, who secured "an armed band of men" and barricaded the road with old wagons and timbers.

So Mr. McInnes remained master of the situation throughout the night; all efforts to parley were in vain. A notice was served upon Construction Superintendent Graves that his company would be held liable for damages if they cut any more trees or destroyed other property fronting on the lands of J. H. McInnes. "Touching his hip significantly," according to the newspaper report, McInnes' son backed up the old man's words and the battle between property owners and railroad was on in full fury.

Now the people rebelled against the use of steam locomotives and the ruination of their most scenic driveway, Corte Madera Avenue, by the dirty, smoking engines. A meeting was held in the office of M. M. O'Shaughnessy in San Francisco, at which the

SIDNEY B. CUSHING

Mr. Cushing was one of the founders and the first president of the Tamalpais Railway. His daughter, Mrs. James Jenkins, has loaned these photographs showing Cushing and, below, his Blithedale Hotel; this building was just outside Mill Valley along the line of the railroad.

—BOTH PHOTOS, MRS. JAMES JENKINS

Mill Valley Property-Owners' Association was formed. Attorneys were contacted and other arrangements made to circumvent the dastardly plans of the mountain road people and the Tamalpais Land & Water Co., which claimed sole power to allow rights-of-way on the lands in question. Mrs. McInnes entered the fray by personally overturning a six-team plow about to dig into the roadway in front of her house, much to the dismay of the operator, who had to retire from the scene in defeat.

On the next day, March 18th, an injunction was obtained by Maurice Windmiller, who owned property on the Avenue and was a member of the Association. The injunction restrained the railroad and its construction company from laying tracks or ties on either Corte Madera or Blithedale Avenues. The papers were rushed from the county seat, San Rafael, to Mill Valley just in time, for the California Construction Co. had pressed that very morning a force of one hundred men to work grading in both the roads named and hauling ties and rails into place. At twelve o'clock this force had been increased and all possible haste was made to rush the road through before legal means were set in motion to stop them. When the injunction papers arrived, the ties were being put in place to receive the rails, and a short delay would have been fatal to the interests of the property owners.

Mr. Windmiller in his complaint alleged that further laying out of the railroad upon these two avenues, making excavations and embankments, would render the lanes almost impassable for vehicles and would interfere with the use of his property, besides greatly depreciating its value. The names of George T. Marsh and M. M. O'Shaughnessy, both influential property owners and San Francisco businessmen, also appeared on the injunction papers. The Property-Owners' Association threatened seven other injunction suits to be filed by different parties owning land along the route.

While the people of Mill Valley were whole-heartedly in favor of the railroad project, they objected to having their roads ruined. It was repeatedly pointed out that the builders of the rail route could run their line a few hundred yards to the east and avoid the avenue entirely. It looked on March 18, 1896, as if this would have to be done if the Tamalpais railroad was to be in running order for the summer, as promised. Strangely enough, while the injunction battle was raging, work was continuing on laying out the road through the property of the aforementioned McInnes, he

— 24 —

having sold two corner lots to the company, plus a right-of-way through his lands on Throckmorton Avenue, opposite the N.P.C. depot. And the cagy McInnes was now a part owner of the road, accepting stock in part payment for the lots and right-of-way.

Already the Mill Valley & Mt. Tamalpais Scenic Railway was referred to in local newspapers as the "Baby Octopus," comparing it to the earlier days of the mighty Southern Pacific. An editorial in the *Marin Press* of March 21st reads in part:

"We appealed, we pleaded, we did all in our power to prevent such a disaster, but the corporations disregarded our advice, and precipitated strife and discord. Trouble being forced upon The People, they will now see that the fangs of corporation greed are drawn; and that the small incisor peeping from the iron jaw of the Baby Octopus is destroyed."

Unperturbed, the Corporation continued construction on other parts of the line, but without assistance from the locomotive. The Shay stood about where the present Mill Valley bus depot is located, and it couldn't be moved across the road until Windmiller's injunction was disposed of. Officials of the railroad tried in vain to have the judge allow them to lay temporary rails across just long enough to get the engine over.

Sidney Cushing, president of the railroad, applied to the Superior Court to set an earlier date for the hearing on the injunction and was successful in having the event moved up one day. In the meantime, the Mill Valley Property-Owners' Association had won every point in the legal battle for possession of the town's roads; not a single stroke of work was being done on the rail line in the disputed area, which included, of course, the first hundred yards of track.

Materials for the construction were piling up everywhere. On the North Pacific Coast Railroad sidetracks in Sausalito were to be seen many cars of rails and ties, which commuters from Mill Valley gloated over on their way to and from work in "the City." There was no place in Mill Valley where the cars could be stored, so it was impossible for the scenic railroad builders to haul the material to men at work up on the mountainside. One thousand ties were unloaded at Sausalito railroad wharf on March 19th from the steamer "Progress"; there they had to sit, and the accumulation was assuming the proportions of a monument to the determination of the people. The company complained that they were losing two hundred dollars a day by the slowing up of the project.

THE EARLIEST EQUIPMENT

When the Mill Valley & Mt. Tamalpais Scenic Ry. went looking for its first coach, it picked up a second-hand cable car from San Francisco's Omnibus line, put it on standard-gauge wheels and changed the name. Below, engines 498 and 2 doublehead an oddly assorted train along the avenues in Mill Valley during the first few months of operation.

But the railroad people were bound to have their day, and have it they did, with a vengeance. During the first day of the two-day hearing on the injunction, much testimony was heard from parties on both sides of the controversy. Construction company, water company and railroad officials argued for the right to build the rail right-of-way in Mill Valley streets, and one of their loudest supporters in Court turned out to be old McInnes again. Opponents of the proposed route were having their say when Court was recessed for the day.

Next morning Windmiller created a sensation with the charge that the company was disobeying the temporary injunction and had yesterday strewn ties, rails and spikes along Corte Madera Avenue. Cushing testified that this dumping of railroad material along the way the night before was done through error of the workmen who did not know the ground. More testimony was thrown in about the kindness of the Tamalpais Land & Water Co., the advantages to be gained in having such a wonderful railroad (witness Steele said he thought the mountain road would bring 100,000 people to live in Mill Valley!); Mr. O'Shaughnessy declared that the flange space between rail and planking would be detrimental to wagon traffic on the roads. Finally, at 3:45 in the afternoon of March 23rd, Judge Angelotti rendered his decision denying the application for an injunction.

A few minutes after the decision was announced in Mill Valley the roadway was alive with workmen. An extra force had been secured in anticipation of a favorable result. In order that the rails might be laid across Throckmorton and Corte Madera Avenues before other injunctions could be obtained, the Scenic Railway Co. determined to push construction as rapidly as possible. The track had to cross Throckmorton, pass through the McInnes property and out on Corte Madera to the powerhouse site, a distance of about eight hundred feet, then on for a total of one and a half miles in such a fashion as to permit the running of a construction train to the front.

Ties and spikes and rails were shortly being thrown around in a grand spectacle of speed, the three hundred track-layers being full of enthusiasm for their project. On through the late afternoon the men sweated furiously under direction of Superintendent Graves. Ties were laid out exactly 22 inches apart; then came brawny laborers with rails, followed by six sturdy spike-drivers. The metallic clank and bang of their sledge hammers

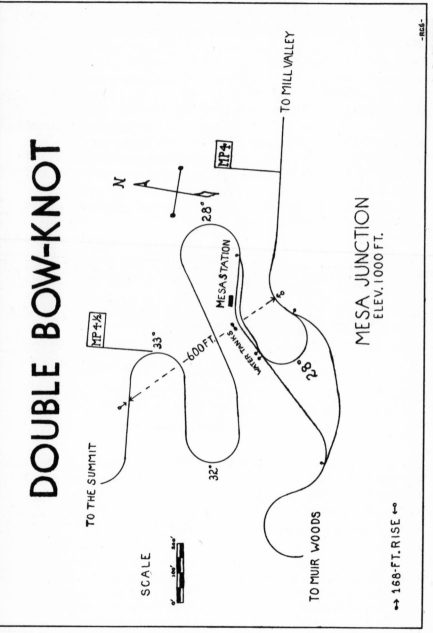

DOUBLE BOW-KNOT

TO THE SUMMIT

MP 4½

33°

600 FT.

32°

28°

N

MESA STATION

WATER TANKS

28°

SCALE

0' 100' 200'

TO MUIR WOODS

MP 4

TO MILL VALLEY

MESA JUNCTION
ELEV. 1000 FT.

← 168-FT. RISE →

—A. C. GRAVES

made even accompaniment to their song, joined into by the throngs of enthusiastic onlookers from all over the county.

On after nightfall the work continued, big bonfires adding their light to the moon's glow to lend dramatic effect to the situation and giving the townspeople a real show in compensation for their loss in Court. About ten in the evening a car was run over part of the line and the track was still lengthening out, when it was discovered that the supply of spikes would not be sufficient to complete the necessary work. In this case the obstacle only served to accelerate the progress, for the superintendent gave orders to spike only into every third tie. The last required rail was laid just before midnight and the fear of being further restrained was over. The company provided a big supper for their men and granted them a half-day's extra pay for the thrilling night's labors. It was reported that in the various construction camps the merry-making went on until morning.

The following day was another momentous one for the new railway. Their borrowed locomotive, No. 498, was steamed up, run out of her temporary shed by engineer Chester Thomas and fireman Kineer under the watchful eyes of a large crowd, and pushed the first carload of material as far as the bridge on the Cushing property. The Shay's shrill whistle saluted the sturdiness of the previous night's trackwork, and then everyone cheered, including McInnes, perched atop the car. The speed was increased on a second trip, setting townspeople inwardly bursting with pride. A switch from the tracks of the North Pacific Coast road had been put in and a third rail laid as far as the projected power-house, so that cars of the narrow gauge could thereafter haul supplies to this point.

Construction of the Mill Valley & Mt. Tamalpais Scenic Railway went on quietly and swiftly for the ensuing five months until its completion in August, 1896. Sniping by the local newspapers continued, of course, but very infrequently. An editorial in the *Marin Press* of March 28th bewailed:

"It has been a serious blow to us to watch the mismanagement which has characterized almost every move. The road is going along and will be completed this summer, and if it can succeed with its present management and second hand machinery, the opinion from engineers and others which we have gone to the expense and trouble to obtain will be reversed."

TRAINS TEST THE MIGHT OF TAMALPAIS

Top left, the first train pauses for a picture en route to the summit with two carloads of newspapermen, August 26, 1896. Only during the first months did engines pull cars upgrade; from then on, the trains were pushed, with engines on the downhill end. Center shows Heisler No. 2 and car on the steepest grade, seven percent, just below the summit. In the lower left, No. 2 makes a picturesque trail of smoke while pushing her one-car train up around one of the bends of the Double Bow-Knot; here the line paralleled itself five times to gain altitude. Above, the "Bull," No. 2, stands in the "yard" at Summit about 1900; the canopy-top, open coaches were painted cream and dark red.

TWO TYPES OF GEARED LOCOMOTIVES

Offset boiler of Shay locomotive clearly shows in this early photo near the top of Tamalpais. Boiler was set left in order to balance weight of the cylinders, all on the right side. Above locomotive has not been positively identified; it is probably No. 1, built 1900 and sold 1904. Below is Heisler No. 2 "Joseph G. Eastland," standing in the streets of Mill Valley; this locomotive's cylinders sloped diagonally under the boiler to drive a central shaft between the wheels. In cab are Engineer Ernest Thomas, killed when this engine turned over on a curve in 1900, and Fireman Thomas H. Bennett.

On August 18, 1896, Superintendent of Construction L. R. Graves drove the last spike of the Mill Valley & Mt. Tamalpais Scenic Railway. Four days later, on the 22nd, the first passenger train made its run to the top of the mountain, an excursion for the people of Mill Valley. Then followed, on August 26th, the official grand opening excursion for members of the press of the San Francisco area, a day carefully prepared for by the management and delightedly reported and long remembered by those present.

About 75 newspapermen left San Francisco at 11:45 on the speedy steamer "San Rafael" and boarded the Mill Valley train at Sausalito. The train drew up at Eastland station in Mill Valley and the guests were greeted by the directors of the mountain road. Then started a round of extreme jollity and happy celebration, carefully calculated to draw from the press enough platitudes to carry this grand new enterprise successfully on its way for some months to come. The mountain train was boarded for the short run to Blithedale, near Cushing's excellent resort hotel. The engine pushed the loaded cars between great redwood trees, crossing the gently flowing waters of the creek, and past luxurious residences, some on disputed Corte Madera Ave.

Out under the trees at Blithedale the scene was set. Two long tables were stretched out, laden with all the fine delicacies of the 'Nineties. In a natural amphitheatre the guests were seated, with tall trees and blue skies overhead, and they drank to the prosperity and long life of the Tamalpais Railway and to the health and wealth of all important personages. A railroad enthusiast would have noted in the setting the gentle sounds of the waiting locomotive, the air pumps keeping brakes steady, the fireman keeping his fire hot with a full head of steam for the long climb ahead, and the conductor and engineer on pins and needles, ready for the most important trip in their lives.

In the grand tradition champagne flowed like water, and the popping of corks added further delight to the pleasantries of the setting. Waiters had been charged not to let the glasses get empty, and they were most faithful in carrying out this duty. Various speakers praised the management, the construction work, the marvelous railroad to the clouds. They foretold the great influx of visitors and residents that Marin County and Mill Valley could expect now that the road was finished — such national groups as Raymond's Excursion Tours would begin sending their cross-country tourists to Tamalpais this very month. G. M. Dodge, the construction engineer, was toasted in especially complimentary terms.

Then Mr. Cushing was called and in a few words invited his guests to come with him to the summit of Tamalpais by railroad and see for themselves the glories in store for travelers on the new scenic railway. The party jumped up with a ringing cheer and hurried to the train. Seats were excitedly chosen, the engine's whistle shrieked its challenge to the mountain, and the ride to the summit commenced.

In and out among the mammoth trees wound the new railroad, over Blithedale Dam, past the Hotel Eastland, "where the ladies waved their handkerchiefs and the gentlemen on the train responded by lifting their hats." The ascent was a gradual one, no grade being steeper than seven percent and the average climb only five percent, while the train twisted and turned around 281 curves from base to summit. Through the forest of redwoods, thousands of years old, passed the train. Crossing a canyon filled with madrones, oaks and laurels, the party looked down upon panoramas of remarkable beauty. At one point the train seemed about to jump off into space, but made a sharp curve around the jutting cliff at the canyon's edge, and a broader view burst upon them, a scene unparalleled for its magnificence.

About halfway up the mountain the train pushed through McKinley Cut and negotiated the "double bow-knot," where the track paralleled itself five times in a few hundred feet in order to gain elevation for a further assault at the lofty peak. The locomotive toiled upwards, over Slide Gulch, past West Point, then right across the southern face of Tamalpais to the top of the mountain. From most summits surrounding peaks shut off the view to some extent, but here was an unbroken vista. Tamalpais rises from the shores of bay and ocean on virtually three sides, and our pioneer mountain railroad excursion party were completely enthralled by the marvels to be seen. Far below them was the ocean to the west, San Francisco to the south, the bay curving around almost to the northeast. Ships under full majestic sail passing through the Golden Gate looked like toy boats from this imposing height. The party had a 150-degree sweep of the Pacific while below them, on the other side of the mountain and less than two direct miles away, lay Mill Valley at the very foot of mighty Tamalpais.

First Locomotives

Both No. 498 and the "Bull," No. 2, changed appearances when the large, spark-arresting diamond stacks were removed in the early 1900's and oil was introduced as fuel. Behind No. 498 is seen the former cable car, which retained its original green paint even when operated on Tamalpais. The "Bull," below, stands at Mill Valley station with engineer "Chick" Garcia to right. Triangular boxes above the front wheels held extra supply of sand to aid in traction and in braking; similar boxes were at rear of engine.

THE TAVERN AT TAMALPAIS

Tamalpais had a series of buildings at its summit; various "Taverns" were built, added to, destroyed, replaced throughout the history of railroad operation. Above is the first Tavern under construction in late 1896; No. 498 stands by to left. Below, after additions, the Tavern looked like this in 1910. Trains struggled the final few hundred feet upgrade and clambered onto level ground just through the arch at the end of the journey. It was no novelty at all to watch the fireman with a bucket of water dousing incipient fires in the wooden arch.

Now Mr. Dodge, in charge of construction, handed out a few statistics of interest to the newspapermen. He told them that the railroad, to reach an altitude of half a mile, was eight and a quarter miles in length, ninety percent of it built in solid rock. The builders had used 22 trestles, but only two through cuts — an advantage for sightseers. The grade contour had been followed, making the 281 curves mentioned, the sharpest having a radius of 72 feet and all taken together adding up to 42 complete circles. The entire route was laid with 57-pound steel rails on redwood ties. Longest stretch of straight track was 413 feet right in the center of the crookedest portion — the double bow-knot.

Fifty-five thousand dollars had been spent in actual construction of the railway, for grading, trestle work and tracklaying, and an additional $80,000 for equipping the line. Rolling stock now consisted of two fine steam engines, the 20-ton Shay No. 498, which had eventually been purchased from the Dollar Lumber Co., and a 30-ton Heisler, No. 2, named "John G. Eastland" and called by everyone "The Bull." There were six open, canopy-top observation cars, one half-closed passenger car, (formerly a San Francisco cable car from the Omnibus line) and two flat-cars. For brakes the railway was equipped with the Westinghouse Automatic Air Brake, a water brake and powerful hand brakes on each locomotive and car. It was planned to schedule an hour and a half for the ascending trip and 45 minutes for the return.

With heads uncovered the gentlemen of the press admired this gorgeous spectacle before them, while considering the engineering marvel which had carried them to it. Mount Diablo reared up to eastward; below to the left was the pretty little town of San Rafael and, close by, the forbidding brick walls of San Quentin prison. Notes were made on the progress of construction work on a summit hotel being built by the scenic railway operators, right where track ended at the top of Tamalpais. Finally it was time to return, and the train twisted back down into the valley, swinging around the curves with ease. The party were safely unloaded and placed on the 5:20 narrow gauge train for San Francisco.

CHAPTER TWO

EARLY OPERATIONS

Operational Methods . . Muir Woods Branch . . On the Road
to Success . . . Extension to Bolinas . . . "Lee Street Local"

Next day, August 27, 1896, regular passenger service began with one round-trip a day scheduled on week days and two on Sundays. Fare for the up-and-back trip was one dollar from Mill Valley and only $1.40 from San Francisco. Despite these attractive fares, the venture was not the immediate financial success it had been expected to be. Various loans had to be paid off, because the road had cost more than anticipated; the trolley plan was soon officially rejected early in 1897. Because of the tightness of the money market, the directors got out of their contracts for electrical machinery as best they could. But President Cushing could report at the beginning of 1897 that "Our credit at the bank has improved, as it is no longer necessary for the President to back the notes of the company." Five thousand passengers were carried in the first five months and the road was found to be easy and safe under steam geared locomotive operation. At the end of a year's operations the directors gratefully acknowledged that over 23,000 passengers had been carried and a profit of $9,992.37 had been earned.

Within the first year the time for a trip to the summit was reduced to an hour and ten minutes. Newspaper and magazine editors in all parts of the United States and western Europe were getting out lengthy articles describing the marvelous engineering feat, the latest improved equipment, the scenes of pastoral beauty and rugged grandeur and prospects including every variety of landscape so beloved of writers of the 'Nineties. All along the lower part of the route fine homes were being built and at the top of the mountain there was a fine tavern — Summit House — up-to-date in style and service and supplying the best of food at comparatively low prices.

The Tamalpais Railroad was hailed as one of the most remarkable pieces of mountain railroad engineering in the country in numerous scientific journals and popular travel monthlies. One of the latter described the Heisler locomotive as "immensely short and stocky, built like a fighter of low, square body, and the very embodiment of strength without grace." The railroad was compared, always favorably, with other mountain lines in the States and Europe, many contending the Tamalpais line surpassed by far all the mountain railroads in this country. One writer, in fact, carried away by the beauty of a particularly clear day, proclaimed the Mill Valley & Mt. Tamalpais Scenic Railway as the "most charming and unique of California's gifts to the World."

In the early part of 1898 the road's second Heisler locomotive, the "S. B. Cushing," was returned to its builders for being "vitally defective in 'cab' arrangement and unsafe for our use," according to the minutes of the directors' meeting of April in that year. The "Cushing" was replaced by a Shay engine, No. 3 "Tamalpais," after another Shay had been purchased and numbered 1 when the company decided to sell old 498 a few years later.

Throughout the year 1898 the railroad barely cleared expenses, according to the president's report of January 19, 1899, because of the combination of a dry year and the war with Spain. During the third full year of operation, from August 1898 to July 1899, the profit was a bare $783.12. Yet the management could see prosperous times and great business ahead, for they authorized an extensive addition to the summit tavern for the early months of 1900. And they added a fine combination car to the rolling stock, in addition to ordering Shay No. 1 for 1900 and the "Tamalpais" for 1901.

The United States Weather Bureau station had been built on West Peak, opposite the upper terminus of the railroad, after much prodding by San Francisco newspapers. The papers had pointed out repeatedly that the station could readily transmit weather news to the city via the railway company's phone line. Moreover, the daily weather balloons and kites would be an added attraction for visitors, and the lookout, viewing the horizon seaward for a distance of 59 miles, would fill a great need watching for shipwrecks and reporting incoming vessels. The railroad itself had a suitable building constructed late in 1898 and leased it to the Weather Bureau for five years at $35 per month. After 1905, two tall, 300-foot wireless towers in conjunction with the station were pointed out as features of the Tamalpais mountain trip. A funicular railway track served the Weather Station, connecting with the mountain railroad at Pieville, just a short distance below the summit terminus.

The picturesque railway's only fatal accident — not a single passenger was killed and only a couple injured in its 34-year existence — occurred on August 22, 1900, when engine No. 2 turned over while coming down the mountain. A steam line in the cab was broken, scalding engineer Chester Thomas very badly. Fireman Joe Paganini crawled from the battered cab and dragged the engineer out; then Paganini carried the burned man all the way up to the tavern on a route that would cause even a seasoned hiker to hesitate. But Thomas died the same day. Cause of the disaster was grease, which had been picked up at the curves and deposited on the ball of the rail the previous day by the flanges of Engine No. 498. The railroad promptly discontinued the use of grease in lubricating wheel flanges on curves, and substituted tiny sprays of water to reduce the friction.

A water line was run under each car, with hose connections between cars and to the engine. When the injector on the engine was pumping water into its boiler, a quarter-inch valve from the discharge was opened to allow a small amount of this feed water to run up into a tank on the roof of the engine cab. From this tank there was always water running through the pipes and hoses to the wheels on the front of the first car, even when the injector was shut off, which was infrequent on that grade. An overflow pipe from the little roof tank would squirt a tiny stream of water to the side of the roadbed in view of the fireman, to let him know that the supply valve was open too much. There was also a small angle cock on the fireman's side of the engine water tank; this cock was always kept open when the locomotive was running to lubricate all of its wheels. The system served admirably for the rest of the road's operations; it was reported in an authoritative British locomotive magazine as a worthwhile innovation that reduced wear of tires, eliminated all wheel squeaking, and kept the wheels and brakeshoes cool on the down trip.

In the operational running of the Mill Valley & Mt. Tamalpais line the decision had early been made to push, rather than pull, cars up the side of the mountain. As a result, the locomotive was always on the lower end of the train and there was absolutely no danger of breakaways. Likewise, ascending sightseers had for the entire journey an unimpeded view of the scenery ahead, with

DOUBLE THREE

First No. 3 was a Heisler named for the road's president, Sidney B. Cushing; it was not satisfactory in service and was returned to the manufacturer soon after delivery. Replacing this engine was Shay No. 3, shown on one of the few trestles about 1907; it ended its years of service on a logging line near Ft. Bragg, where it was scrapped in 1929.

neither locomotive nor smoke to obstruct the scenic beauties of Nature. Trains were limited to three or four cars so that there would be no danger of shoving a car off the track on sharp curves by having too much weight up front. Occasional specials had up to five cars from time to time, but they were few and far between. Technically, only three were authorized by the California Railroad Commission.

Toward the close of 1901 representatives of the Lima Locomotive Company were approached with the idea of turning in Shay No. 498 on a newer model. San Francisco's Lima agent told Mr. Cushing that his company could allow only a thousand or fifteen hundred dollars for her and advised them to attempt to sell the engine themselves, probably for a great deal more money. And the company did sell the 498 to a logging railway in Washington. In that state she served faithfully on four subsequent lumber railroads before eventually being broken up for scrap.

Shay engine No. 4 was ordered in April 1903 for $6900, to be delivered on July 15th, in time for the summer rush. No. 3 had turned out to be so satisfactory that the 4-spot was of the same weight and capacity, though considerably taller and an oil burner from the start. Her weight was 23 tons, with three ten-by-ten cylinders and 28-inch wheels. Shay No. 1 was sold at the end of 1904 for $2250 and another, No. 5, came to the Tamalpais Railway in 1906.

First dividend to stockholders was declared at the directors' meeting of July 17, 1902, and it amounted to one dollar per hundred-dollar share of stock, payable on the 11th of August. A second of the same amount followed in three months, and further one-dollar dividends were paid quarterly until November, 1905, at which time the payment was raised to $1.25 per share. This five-percent rate was to continue with such periodic certainty, except for four years immediately following on the heels of the 1906 San Francisco disaster, that newspapers called it the "regular quarterly five-percent dividend."

Happily enough, the railroad management did not start out sacrificing maintenance to pay dividends. A progressive system of filling in trestles was followed annually, until nearly the entire route was on solid ground. New and better equipment was purchased as required; grading of the entire route was improved through the years. In 1904 another tavern was constructed on the line, this one at West Point, where the railroad looked down upon

The inn at West Point was literally surrounded by the mountain railroad, as tracks approached from below and curved away at upper right. Below is Engine No. 4 and train of gravity cars posed for a panoramic photograph in 1920 at Mesa station, the half-way point also known as the Double Bow-Knot.

—A. C. GRAVES-PENNINGTON COLLECTION

—MARVIN T. MAYNARD

ALONG THE PICTURESQUE MUIR WOODS BRANCH

Engine No. 4 stops at the edge of this forest of massive redwoods, one of the most lovely spots in America. The branch ran from Bow-Knot, was over two miles long.

the Pacific before making a horseshoe turn back and up to the summit. At this point passengers could change to a stage for Bolinas, and it was to be a busy station in later years when train-load after trainload of passengers alighted here to walk to the Tamalpais Mountain Theatre.

All engines were fitted out to burn oil instead of wood by 1902, thus effecting a large fuel saving and cutting down on the fire hazard in late summer months. The Tamalpais was one of the first railroads in the world to change over to oil-burning locomotives; its owners and officers were quick in the early years to take advantage of any improvement that would add to their earnings or improve the beauty and value of the region they served. Thus it was that the branch line to Muir Woods, with a lovely inn at the terminus, was planned and constructed during 1906 and opened in the spring of the following year.

Before this time, what was to become nationally beloved Muir Woods had been called Redwood Canyon, and was a remote retreat accessible only over a narrow stagecoach road. During 1905 Mr. William Kent (1864-1928) of Kentfield in Marin County, later a member of Congress (1911-1917), purchased this canyon in the interest of preserving the natural beauties of the Tamalpais region for public benefit. Then Kent went to the mountain railroad directors with the proposition that they build a spur line to some point near the canyon and he would construct a fine, modern hotel at the same place, at a cost of $60,000. This hotel and accessories Kent agreed to rent to the railway for a period of twenty years, and would allow them full occupancy of the entire tract of six hundred acres for five years. After that time, he would be allowed to take certain portions to the north and east for subdivision and sale, these portions having no value in connection with the features of Redwood Canyon itself. Kent would also get ten percent of all passenger fares into the area up to $3000, and after that, five percent.

Upon surveying the route, the railroad company found that a branch of approximately two and a half miles would be needed, the grade from Mesa (Double Bow-Knot) being four percent, from Mine Ridge to the hotel site, six percent. Still to be determined was the question of a right-of-way over land of the North Coast Water Company. This company did not want to dispose of their holdings unless Kent agreed to sell them certain of his lands, but eventually an understanding was reached and the branch was built, after necessary changes in the Articles of Incorporation of the railway had been made.

Fireman on the first train into Muir Woods, in early 1907, was Roy D. Graves, well-known San Franciscan, who has contributed photographs and information to numerous historical works on transportation and Californiana. His engineer was Jake Johnson, participating in another Tamalpais milestone. During the rest of 1907, however, the branch was not fully operated by the company. In the first place, Johnson and Graves had been sent down the new branch without any assurance that the engine would be able to push a loaded train out. The luxuriant weed growth had not hindered them, fortunately, and the run was made without incident. But there began a tremendous increase of Sunday travel to the mountain during the summer of that year; rolling stock was taxed to capacity. Also, no building had been constructed in the woods as yet, owing to high labor and material costs. Some passengers managed to make the trip coasting down by gravity car, however, and this appears to have been the first occasion for using these unique vehicles — these Tamalpais gravities which are associated affectionately in the hearts of nostalgic travelers with all that is "good" in the old days.

In November 1907 the water company commenced suit to condemn a piece of land in the heart of the grove for reservoir purposes. Mr. Kent, to circumvent this move and to carry out his original intent of preserving this lovely spot intact, deeded three hundred acres to the United States Government as a National Monument. It was the first such offer that Congress was able to accept under a new law. President Theodore Roosevelt, on January 4, 1908, officially took title to the land in the name of the United States, and the monument was named Muir Woods, in honor of John Muir, the California naturalist. Then Kent, his original agreement with the railroad proving impossible to carry out, offered to sell to the company 190 acres of land adjoining the government reserve, on which they could erect their own inn or hotel. This was entirely suitable to the company. It ordered in the same month another Shay engine, No. 7, and three new open passenger coaches. To finance all this extension and enlargement of facilities, bonded indebtedness of the company was increased from $100,000 to $200,000.

MT. TAMALPAIS

DO

NOT FAIL TO

TAKE

THIS

TRIP

THE

GRANDEST

MOUNTAIN

RAILWAY

RIDE

ON EARTH

MILL VALLEY AND
MT. TAMALPAIS

SCENIC RAILWAY
"THE CROOKEDEST RAILROAD IN THE WORLD"

MOUNTAIN RAILROADS
LENGTH OF DIFFERENT ROADS AND FARE CHARGED

			Round Trip
MT. WASHINGTON	New Hampshire 3	miles long	$4.00
PILATUS	Switzerland 3	miles long	$2.40
SCHYNIGIE PLATTE	Switzerland	4½ miles long	$2.00
RIGI VITZNAU	Switzerland	4½ miles long	$2.10
MONTE GENEROSE	Switzerland	5½ miles long	$2.00
GORNER GRAT	Switzerland	5¾ miles long	$3.60
MT. LOWE RY.	California	8½ miles long	$1.75
(From Los Angeles to Alpine Tavern, 21 miles, Fare $2.50)			

"The Crookedest Railroad in the World"

MT. TAMALPAIS	California	8½ miles long	$1.50
(From San Francisco, 20½ miles, Fare $1.90)			
PIKE'S PEAK	Colorado	8½ miles long	$5.00

ROUND TRIP   SAN FRANCISCO

To MT. TAMALPAIS and return - - $1.90

To MUIR WOODS and return - - -   1.90

To MT. TAMALPAIS and MUIR WOODS - 2.90

Trains Run Every Day in the Year

VIA SAUSALITO FERRY
(NORTHWESTERN PACIFIC)

Union Ferry Depot - - - Foot of Market Street

SAN FRANCISCO, CALIFORNIA

TICKET OFFICES

SAUSALITO FERRY
(Foot of Market Street)
TELEPHONE KEARNY 4980

874 MARKET ST.
(Flood Building)
TELEPHONE DOUGLAS 4407

GENERAL OFFICE, MILL VALLEY, CAL.

SEE DAILY PAPERS FOR TIME TABLE

HOW TO SEE CALIFORNIA IN A DAY

Take the Sausalito Ferry from Union Ferry Depot, foot of Market Stree., San Francisco, and go to the summit of MT. TAMALPAIS, via the Mill Valley and Mt. Tamalpais Scenic Railway. A sail on San Francisco Bay, a ride on "The Crookedest Railroad in the World," a continuous ever-changing Panorama of Mountains, Valleys, Ocean, Bays, Cities and Towns, as you gradually ascend to a height of half a mile above the surrounding country. You see more from Mt. Tamalpais than from any other mountain peak in the world; on a clear day the snow-capped Sierra Nevada mountains 155 miles distant can be plainly seen and Mt. Shasta rising nearly three miles high and 300 miles away, can be discerned. The Mt. Tamalpais trip gives one the best idea of locations in California, and you can say with truth after having made this trip that you have seen nearly the whole of California.

—MARVIN T. MAYNARD

It was proposed to run a shuttle train service from the Bow-Knot to Muir Woods on weekdays, starting early in the summer of 1908. On Sundays a special train was to make seven trips between Mill Valley and the redwood grove. At the same time it was decided to spend $150,000 on the big hotel at the woods, in view of the government's new ownership of the place and the greatly increased travel. A 25-passenger gasoline railcar was purchased in 1909 for the shuttle service on this branch. It had a locally-made body, with sturdy Stoddard-Dayton engine and two speeds in both directions.

With these improvements and the backing of their twelve-year record of safely conveying passengers up and down the mountain, the Mill Valley and Mt. Tamalpais Scenic Railway entered upon a period of well earned prosperity. It was a time bubbling over with all sorts of grandiose schemes for expansion and further progress in all directions. The road carried thousands of passengers from all over the world, including all the famous travelers of the time. The novelist, Gertrude Atherton, who had spent her childhood in the shadow of Tamalpais, was one of the greatest boosters for the railroad. She spent several weeks each year at the summit. Susan B. Anthony spoke at the tavern; President Teddy Roosevelt had the region often in his mind as evidenced in correspondence with William Kent and an extended visit by Mrs. Roosevelt and her party.

The national Raymond Excursion officials in their newspaper interviews proclaimed the trip far superior to the Mount Lowe excursion in southern California — and apparently their guests agreed with them. What could be more soothing to San Francisco ears than such a comparison? Delegates to all San Francisco conventions made the journey over the Bay and up to the Tamalpais Summit by scenic railway a part of their agenda. Doctors, sailors, businessmen from the Northwest, Delta Upsilons, astronomers, governors from a score of states, foreign dignitaries and visiting royalty — all traveled the crookedest railroad in the world, negotiated the thrilling Double Bow-Knot, dined at the tavern and were coasted down to Muir Woods in the gravity cars.

At its 1910 meeting, closing the fiscal year on June 30th, the company management was pleased to report big gains for the year. The grand total of passengers carried was up seventeen and a half percent over the previous twelve months; new earnings for the year were $22,549.37, and still the equipment and road were in first-class condition, the indebtedness to the bank had been paid off, and various improvements had been made to the Tavern of Tamalpais and to Muir Inn.

In this same year of 1910 company president, C. F. Runyon, entered into the pioneering spirit of the times and offered a reward of one thousand dollars to the first aviator who should fly his plane from San Francisco and encircle the summit of Tamalpais. It seems to have been about this time, too, that the company motto, "Crookedest Railroad in the World," began to be loosely bandied about in the newspaper columns. Inevitably, a visitor would be introduced to one of the company officials of the "Crookedest Railroad" and would snort, as the papers reported it, "Don't want to meet anyone connected with the Southern Pacific!" A variation came up in occasional columns describing the scenic railway; the reporter would faithfully recite "Crookedest Railroad in the World" and hastily add in the same sentence, "not in any way connected with a Harriman road, either."

The profit-making disposition of the mountain railroad became especially evident in the yearly increases in net income, from 1909 to 1912. As is customary, such a trend led the directors to larger plans, and in 1911 there came into full bloom another scheme for extension of the railroad to Bolinas and that general area on the shores of the Pacific, northwest of Tamalpais. The original plans to build on from the summit when the line was first laid down had not borne fruit — they were highly impractical. However, in 1902 the railroad company had spent $5000 in building a wagon road from West Point — about three-quarters of the way up the mountain and facing the ocean — to the settlement of Willow Camp on Bolinas Beach, not far from the village of that name. Thereby, the rail line was able to get revenue from the carriage of passengers bound for Bolinas, trains meeting a stagecoach at West Point House. Now, after the passage of nine more years, the railroad definitely planned to extend a branch right down most of this same stage road to Willow Ranch, thence on to Bolinas. Here would be eventually established "one of the largest beach and vacation resorts in the northern part of California." Contracts were let on March 24, 1911, for the construction of five miles of approximately four percent grade in a very picturesque area. The company announced that they proposed to erect at Willow Camp an immense hotel on the high bluff, commanding a wide sweep of the Pacific.

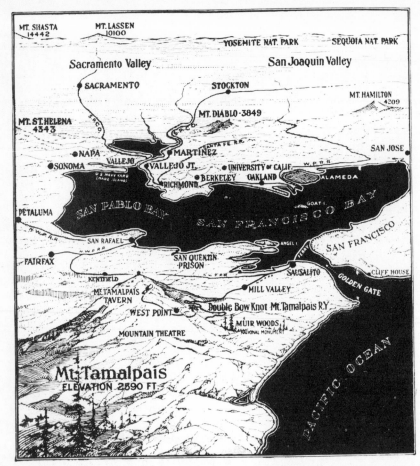

Above, a "bird's-eye-view" diagram issued by the Mt. Tamalpais & Muir Woods Ry. to show places advertised as visible from the lofty summit. Below, the homely "Bull" waits leisurely in the early afternoon sun at Mill Valley. When the narrow-gauge North Shore train arrives from Sausalito, she will start backwards up the slopes of Tamalpais.

—VERNON J. SAPPERS

THE GRAVES BROTHERS

Both Roy and Cliff ("Hank") had grown up with the "Mountain Road," so it was natural that they would get their teen-age jobs working on the line. That's proud Roy, fireman, leaning on No. 5 above, in 1907. His brother Cliff is the brakeman in center of the photo to right, taken 1910. Jake Johnson appears as engineer in both views; Wesley Armager is fireman in the lower picture.

RAILROAD ODDITIES

These three views of "self-propelled" vehicles of Tamalpais show the ingenuity employed by this railroad to take advantage of the line's natural features. Gravity cars, left, coasted from the summit; two shown here are nearing Muir Woods Inn in the giant redwoods. At right is the old "Booster" which operated by its own small steam engine. Below, motor No. 2, built in Mill Valley shops around a Stoddard-Dayton engine, could run 25-30 miles per hour up the mountain.

—MRS. JAMES JENKINS

—T. G. WURM

At the very tip of Tamalpais was erected the "Marine Exchange," a sort of observation station to which tourists climbed from the train. Below, West Point in a view looking southeastward; behind the tavern is a stable where Bolinas stage horses were kept. That's the stage road running out of picture at lower left, going down the western slope to the edge of the Pacific Ocean only four miles away.

—A. C. GRAVES-PENNINGTON COLLECTION

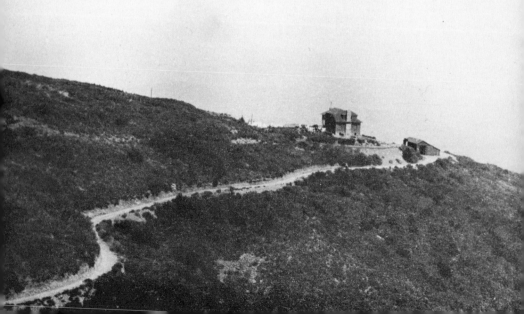

THE PEAKS OF TAMALPAIS

West Peak in the foreground above, featured two 300-ft. wireless towers. In the distance can be seen the U. S. Weather Bureau station and Tamalpais Tavern, nestled near the top of East Peak. The wireless station was served by its own funicular railway, which joined the mountain railroad on the open ridge just down from the summit.

VARIETIES IN ROLLING STOCK

Open coach No. 9 above and, below, a similar car that was closed in at the company's own shops. These coaches were painted a dark red, almost maroon, to match most of the locomotives. Connecting hoses at the ends of the cars were for air (brakes), steam (heat) and water (to cool wheels).

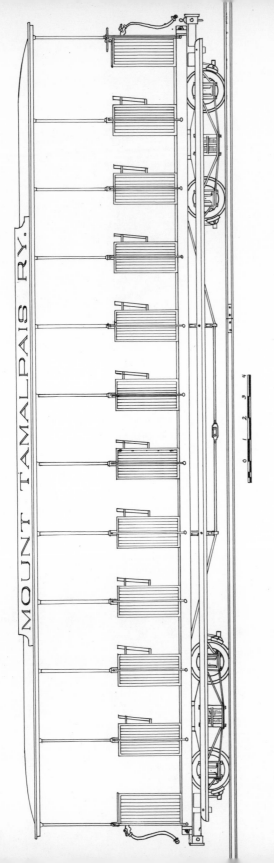

Passenger coach drawn to scale by C. A. Graves. This was the type of car most commonly used in trains.

—ROY D. GRAVES

Muir Woods Branch left the mainline at Mesa, the Double Bow-Knot, shown in the photo above. Engine No. 4 is stopped down by the water tanks, pausing in her backward journey up the mountain. Tank car at one time carried water to the summit. Below, No. 3 at the end of Muir Woods Branch, stopped in front of the inn at the edge of the canyon forest. Pipes sticking from top of smokestack are part of the mechanism of the "Porcupine" feedwater heater described on page 95.

—A. C. GRAVES-PENNINGTON COLLECTION

HEIGH-HO AND AWAY WE GO

Gravity Car No. 15 leaves the summit tavern for the thrilling glide down the slopes of mighty Tamalpais. What a grand feeling to float effortlessly around the curves of the Double Bow-Knot, with spectacular views on every side and the redwood canyons below!

BRANCH LINE TO BOLINAS

The distant peak towered over Bolinas stage road, but the four horses had only to reach West Point Tavern, barely visible above the lead horse. From there travelers took the Mt. Tamalpais railroad down to Mill Valley and connection for San Francisco. It was down this road that the scenic railway management proposed in 1911 to run a five-mile branch to Dipsea Inn, below, and Bolinas, on the shores of the Pacific.

San Francisco newspapers of Monday, March 27, 1911, announced construction as starting that morning; but April 17th papers were still giving the news that construction would start "at once." Then, on April 20th, the line was apparently underway with construction gangs working at West Point, some crossties already on the ground; the citizens of Bolinas were hard at work raising money for a drawbridge to bring the railroad right into town. President Runyon now tossed caution to the winds and came out with an announcement of grandiose new plans to build a direct line, straight from Mill Valley to Dipsea and Bolinas, involving heavy grading, fills and two long tunnels through the ridges of Tamalpais. This entirely new scheme was estimated publicly to cost $800,000, and it was designed to put the people of San Francisco on the beach in seventy minutes, or just twenty minutes from Mill Valley. Here was the mountain road's answer to the Ocean Shore Railroad, which ran south from the city to "Reach the Beaches."

After Runyon's announcement, however, this fancy idea never was publicly mentioned again, and the next reference we find states that the original extension down the stagecoach road would be in operation within ten weeks, using gasoline railcars instead of mountain locomotives and coaches. Each railcar would have a capacity of twenty passengers, and gravity-type trailers would be used to accommodate as many more, if traffic warranted. The gasoline car service to Muir Woods, and another trial in Mill Valley local service, had met with some success. The company felt it could make such an operation pay, even with the necessarily small initial business they would draw. The entire extension could be built and equipped for $38,000, including $7500 for the motorcars and trailers.

This Bolinas Branch of the Mill Valley & Mt. Tamalpais Scenic Railway was never completed; apparently not a foot of track was ever laid upon the few ties that were in place. No mention is made in the contemporary newspapers as to the reason for abandonment of the plan, but perhaps the building of an auto road from Mill Valley to the Bolinas area gave the directors warning of future losses and they quietly killed the project. They were anything but dormant, however; they had other projects, and plenty of them. The year 1912 saw the railroad management considering the building of a huge, 300-passenger inclined elevator railway to carry passengers from the railway's inn and terminus at Muir Woods,

Lee Street Local

Engine No. 6 (above), with coach, performed Mill Valley's streetcar service for years, running between the depot and Lee St., at the head of Blithedale Canyon. Kissell Kar No. 3 took over (below) in 1916. No. 6 spent her last days in 1935 building Monterey breakwater (right).

1906 in Mill Valley

The local train, engine No. 6, waits at Lee Street for passengers (right). At the other end of the one-mile run was Mill Valley depot (below). Here Engineer Bonner Whitcomb, left, and 17-year-old Conductor Cliff Graves pose beside their beloved "dinkey," shortly after the 6-Spot went into service.

—CLIFF GRAVES

—ROY D. GRAVES

The Station at Mill Valley

Light smoke from the narrow-gauge passenger train drifts up from the platform in this view (above) taken from the first slopes of Tamalpais. The mountain trains stopped to the left (below) with engines ready to push off for the lofty peak as connecting trains arrived from Sausalito.

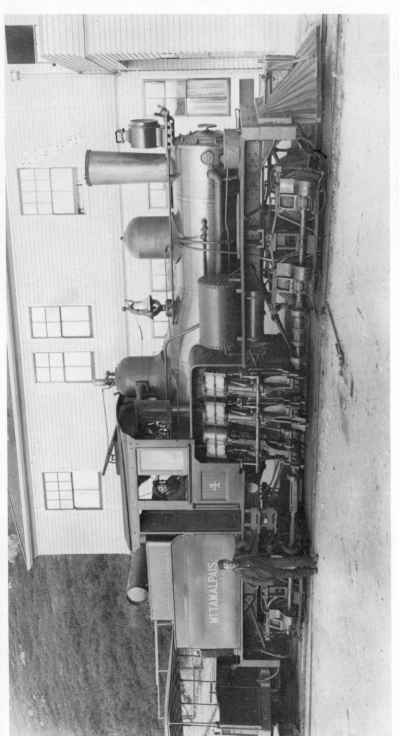

THE GRACEFUL SHAY

If ever a Shay-type locomotive could be called graceful, No. 4 would qualify. Here she stands in a new coat of dark red paint, at the summit, April 20, 1907. In the cab window is engineer Frank Clark; Roy Graves, fireman, stands proudly beside the tender; the lettering was done in gold leaf.

—ALL PHOTOS, A. C. GRAVES-PENNINGTON COLLECTION

MUIR WOODS VIGNETTES Opposite page shows Park Ranger O'Rourke in the office at Muir Woods Inn. The party of sightseers are posed in a gravity car at the end of track in Muir Woods. The third view opposite shows engine No. 3 approaching Muir Woods Inn with the morning train. The Muir Woods gravity "train" left the summit (above) just after lunch. This early view shows Bill Thomas, famed master mechanic and later superintendent, with his hand on side of car to right. In the last view, engine No. 4 comes through Mine Ridge Cut, with pipe line crossing overhead.

down four hundred feet to the floor of the gorgeous redwood canyon itself. Approval of the California Railroad Commission was actually sought for this improvement, and at the same time the railway asked for permission to convert its local services in Mill Valley to electric trolley operation.

The local services in the town of Mill Valley consisted of a train running up and down Blithedale Canyon and connecting with all trains of the North Shore Railroad, standard-gauge electric interurban successor to the old N.P.C. This "Lee Street Local," as it was affectionately known in the valley, had been put into operation in the spring of 1905 with the company's first gasoline railcar, an open Thomas Flyer with side seats for six, known as "Black Maria." The president had noted in his January, 1906, annual message that "it has paid running expenses, and was found to be to our advantage in many ways. We have ordered a small locomotive, with which the run can be made more economically, and we hope to make the service produce a direct revenue this year." The small locomotive was a little four-wheel, saddle-tank steamer numbered 6, built by the H. K. Porter Company with pretty, ornamental capped stack and a generously proportioned cab.

Going into service in 1906, Engine No. 6 with its one wooden coach performed a streetcar-type service up the canyon to Lee Street station, over a mile from the heart of town. Scores of residents, both old and new, were thus enabled to make direct connections with electric trains for San Francisco and to ride into Mill Valley for shopping. The moderate five-cent fare attracted a substantial patronage and the tiny engine with its small combination coach was the pride and joy of every child in town. Bonner Whitcomb and Joe Marshall were the regular engineers; conductor was usually a man named Courtney or young Cliff Graves, whose brother, Roy, was a fireman on the railroad at the same time. The contemplated plan to electrify this portion of the Tamalpais Railway and make it a true trolley service failed to materialize, since 1912 was a rather bad year. The steam train later became a luxury and the management went back to gasoline railcar service in more modern form. Motor No. 3 was a 1916 Kissel Kar with eight flanged wheels — a vehicle that really rolled, according to old-time employees.

The Kissel was a big sight when delivered new in Mill Valley. A rugged passenger-carrying body had been built in San Fran-

THE CLASSIC POSE AT THE TAVERN OF TAMALPAIS

A special party of Shriners and friends prepares for the descent behind engine No. 7, about 1915. Perhaps it was the Fourth of July — whatever the occasion, No. 7 carried flags on the pilot beam and headlight. Note the small cylindrical tank atop the engine's cab. This held a reserve supply of water to keep the wheels lubricated and cool.

cisco, fitted with every comfort, clean and attractively painted; she became the "Pullman" of the mountain road's motor cars. Power was transmitted by a double chain, four-wheel drive, with four speeds, capable of twelve miles per hour uphill. Logically enough, this became the car used to carry special private parties up the mountain, replacing the quaint four-wheel "Booster," a gravity car with upright steam boiler and a canopy top — indeed a wonderful railway carriage. Jam brakes were mounted on the pony truck of the Kissel Kar, and an extra bag of sand carried on mountain journeys, for she tended to run away on rough track. Shop crews drilled holes through the floor, laid a common kitchen funnel handy to the sandbag and a plumber's "cleanout" to get damp sand moving down onto the track so the brakes could take hold. Water was used, as on the steam trains, to keep the wheels cool and lubricated on turns.

Even with all these attractive features — or, perhaps, because of them — the Kissel Kar never quite took the place of the little steam local train in the hearts of residents. They maintained the gas car had an unpredictable temper on cold mornings and soon lost the confidence of commuters with connections to make. Little engine No. 6 was sold for $1400 in 1915 to a construction company and saw service in the Monterey area and other parts of California before being stored at the Atkinson Construction Company yard in East Oakland and finally scrapped during the Second World War.

But back in 1912 when the company was considering electrifying their Lee Street Local, many newspapers jumped to the conclusion that electric cars would supplant the quaint steam trains on the entire mountain railroad, and loud was the wailing of the press over the passing of the "chuggy steam engines" when the "electricizing" would take place. As a matter of fact, some newspapers even exaggerated the inclined elevator plan for Muir Woods into a route to the very summit of the mountain! The State Railroad Commission, as if to settle all confusion and speculation, cut the railroad's request to issue 1500 shares down to 869, and apparently by that move put the damper on both schemes for good.

About 1910, at the Summit of Tamalpais, canopy-top coach No. 8 (above) disgorges her crowd of happy travelers after the awesome climb from Mill Valley. Sightseers could walk around the peak on a level boardwalk or climb a few hundred feet (below) to the observation station at the peak's tip.

SEE THE **COMET**
FROM
Mt. Tamalpais
EXCURSION
Each Evening during the Month of May
Via SAUSALITO FERRY

Leaving SAN FRANCISCO 4:45 P.M.
Arriving Mt. Tamalpais 6:40 P. M.

Leaving MT. TAMALPAIS 9:50 P.M.
Arriving San Francisco 11:42 P. M.

DINNER AT TAVERN OF TAMALPAIS
A LA CARTE
AT POPULAR CITY PRICES

Mt. Tamalpais was the ONLY POINT from which the Comet was visible on Monday evening. Situated half a mile high it is usually above the fogs of San Francisco Bay. From now on the conditions will be better than they have been as the moon is getting out of the way, rising later each evening. Ask any of the 600 who made the trip on last Monday evening and they will tell you

DO NOT FAIL TO MAKE THE TRIP

Samples of company
advertising, courtesy
California-Nevada R.R.
Historical Society

Unusual Weather!

Engines Nos. 8 and 5 to the rescue! Mount Tamalpais snows seldom last overnight; in many years not a trace falls all winter. January, 1922, however, was different — a "real" snowfall, improvised snowplows on the Shays, shoveling scenes at the tavern (below). Two locomotives (right) set out to pull free the train with snowplow, which failed to do its job.

—BOTH PHOTOS, A. C. GRAVES-PENNINGTON COLLECTION

CHAPTER THREE

A NEW NAME

*Gravity Cars . . . A Day on the Mountain . . . Forest Fires
. . . Prosperity Wanes . . . Bill Thomas . . .*

In order to be in a better position to enlarge the scope of their
business, the directors in early 1913 petitioned for permission to
form a new company, to be known as the Mt. Tamalpais & Muir
Woods Railway. The latter was to take over all property and
operations of the old Mill Valley & Mt. Tamalpais Scenic, and was
to be incorporated with a capital stock of $500,000, an increase
of $300,000 over the old company. One of the projects stated in
the application was again the extension of the line to Bolinas by
the same old route via West Point and the stage road, "and to
other points in Marin County." The annual statement for 1912
had shown a total net profit of $21,781.44, with a surplus of
$124,824.18; the railway portion of the company, as separate from
the taverns and inn and the telephone line, had by itself cleared
$39,677 over operating expenses.

Under the new corporation plans were announced for construction of a new engine house and shop in Mill Valley, near the
mouth of Corte Madera Canyon, and not far from the center of
town. New equipment was purchased — additional coaches and
several gravity cars. The new Mt. Tamalpais & Muir Woods Railway started business with six steam locomotives, including Shays
No. 3, 4, 5, 7 and 8, and the small 0-4-0t No. 6. The company was
operating nineteen open, canopy-top passenger coaches of wooden
construction, two half-enclosed and two entirely enclosed coaches,
one flatcar, two gasoline motor cars, and sixteen gravity cars.
Coaches were equipped with Westinghouse Air Brakes, all cars
having a special two-way check valve permitting the operation of
train brakes by either automatic or straight air.

The gravity cars were the pride and joy of the mountain road's
master mechanic, Bill Thomas, who had had much to do with
planning and designing them. Those fortunate enough to have
coasted down the slopes of Tamalpais by gravity were quite fond

of the little cars, and there are thousands who still cherish the memory of such a novel journey. Their first thought at the mention of old days on the mountain is of the gravity car ride from the summit down to Muir Woods or the direct run to Mill Valley. It was a fairly steady downgrade all the way, except for one flat spot at Fern Canyon; at that place five curves of average radius and a sixth of special sharpness tended to slow the cars down. It was necessary for the "gravity man" to "let 'er roll" approaching Fern Canyon, so the car would get up enough excess speed to coast over the flat place without stalling.

Tamalpais gravity cars received their initial prominence in connection with the opening of service into Redwood Canyon, later Muir Woods. These cars were small four-wheelers, carrying thirty people in wooden seats running right across the cars, one behind the other. The operator, locally known as the "gravity man," was in charge at his front, right-hand seat. He operated a set of strong double brakes with the aid of a huge handle beside him. A speed of ten to twelve miles per hour was averaged in gliding silently down the hill. One can readily imagine how thrilling it was, this wonderful roller coaster ride with the world-renowned beauties of the Tamalpais country and vast panoramas of California scenery unfolding at every turn. There was the deep pleasure of rolling softly through groves of tall, peaceful redwoods, completely detached from the noise and bustle of everyday life.

Just the mention of the Tamalpais gravity cars brought memories of a moonlight ride down the mountain railroad to a librarian who had been approached for references on the line. We can gain some idea of the wonders of this trip from old guidebook descriptions and books on the marvels of Marin. Pieced together, they form a pretty clear picture of the setting, in the language of another generation — moon flickering through the high branches onto sparkling shrubbery and massive tree trunks, mottling the ground with patches of silver. A tiny brook glistens for a moment in the light and is gone; ferns, dogwood and other blooms overhang the tracks in a canopy of beauty, with stars, perhaps a fleecy cloud or two, overhead. Night noises of crickets, tree toads, cicadas blend perfectly with an occasional sound from the rolling wheels on a curve. Such is truly a scene worth remembering for a lifetime.

SUNDAY TRIP TO TIP OF TAMALPAIS

(Above) The photo of Nos. 3, 5, and 7 with trains is typical of "Tamalpias panoramas" taken for the sightseers to take home as souvenirs. The ferry slips at Sausalito are approached at the end of a 35-minute ride (upper left) from San Francisco; Northwestern Pacific's "Cazadero" to right with Mount Tamalpais beyond. (Center left) The mountain train at Mill Valley depot with two types of N. W. P. electric cars. (Below) Engine No. 3's train halts for a moment at West Point Tavern to exchange passengers with the Bolinas stage. Last stop (lower left) is at Tavern of Tamalpias, showing here the three-track "railroad yard" scooped out of the side of the mountain.

—BERTRAM H. WARD

Railroad Men Pose for Their Pictures

Engines Nos. 4 and 5 pose with their crews. The view at the Double Bow-Knot (above) shows Conductor John Patterson, Fireman Joe Ferrari and Engineer Jake Johnson; date: 1918. Below, left to right, are Brakeman A. Palazzi, two unidentified figures, Engineer Joe Marshall (in white), Fireman E. Johnson, and unidentified trainman. Coach 22, behind engine, resembled a streetcar. (At left) Engine No. 7 at the summit. This engine was used for several months in 1916-17 on the Hetch Hetchy Railroad in the Sierra Nevada Range.—A. C. GRAVES PHOTO

—A. C. GRAVES-PENNINGTON COLLECTION

It was the usual custom on a day's outing to Tamalpais for a happy young couple, or the city father with his throng, to catch the morning ferry at the north end of the Ferry Building and cross San Francisco Bay to Sausalito. From there, by electric train of the Northwestern Pacific, it was only a few minutes to Mill Valley. The friendly-looking mountain train would be waiting beside the platform, just across from the interurban, with two or three open cars, and the Shay locomotive breathing warmly into the clear air. Up to the summit they would go, the engine running backwards and pushing steadily all the way. Perhaps lunch would be taken on the glassed-in veranda of the Tavern — their prices were reasonable and the food at times excellent — looking down on San Francisco, thirteen miles away, the bay and the Golden Gate. Right below on the mountainside could be seen a train of diminutive cars winding its tortuous course in and around the hundreds of curves, the toy engine fighting every inch of the steep incline and panting like a Dipsea cross-country runner with its Herculean efforts to reach the summit.

After lunch it was "All Aboard for the Gravity Ride to Muir Woods," leaving behind the faint-hearted for the more sedate train ride down. Branching off the main line at the Bow-Knot, the carefully packed gravities proceeded one by one in solemn procession toward the glories of the redwood forest. By easy grades the cars coasted along the sides of mountain canyons, through laurel, fir, oak, madrone and other varieties of tree growth, finally stopping at Muir Inn on a sunny slope overlooking the very redwoods themselves, relics of past centuries. Late in the afternoon the return was made to Mill Valley by steam train, the engine pushing its canopy-topped coaches ahead up the hill and hauling behind a string of empty gravities. At Mesa station, the Bow-Knot again, the tracks formed a "Y" with the Muir Woods Branch as the tail and the curved main line running across the ends. So it was simplicity itself for the engine to push its loaded coaches from the branch up onto the curved Bow-Knot, then reverse and head for Mill Valley, the engine remaining always below the cars on the grade.

Many good stories of the old railroad are centered on the famous Double Bow-Knot itself, where the tracks paralleled themselves five times on a broad shoulder of Tamalpais, in order to gain elevation for the final charge to the summit. When Cliff Graves was conductor on steam runs from the peak down to the

Woods, he'd have to throw a switch at the Bow-Knot for the train to get onto Muir Woods Branch. Cliff would be riding the last car coming down and would drop off unobserved at the upper part of the Bow-Knot, walk a few hundred feet downhill through the brush, and would throw the switch and be waiting when his train appeared round the bend from uphill. This feat never failed to amaze tourists traveling the line for the first time.

The story is told of a thrilling night-time gravity ride by Vollie Thoney, who resides in Mill Valley. He went to work for the road in 1920, sometimes acting as engineer, at other times working in the shops or keeping the refrigerator and player piano operating at the Summit Tavern. One moonlit night Thoney had been repairing something at the tavern and started home to Mill Valley at two in the morning by gravity car. Coming into the level place at Fern Canyon he had gained all the speed he could, without the added weight of passengers, to ensure reaching the down grade beyond. Speeding around the curve he suddenly spotted a deer on the track ahead, standing erect in the pale light of the moon. Thoney was unable to stop the car in so short a distance, even if he wanted to. He hollered and beat a tattoo on the car's gong, but the deer stood petrified. Almost in the same instant the gravity struck, as Thoney dived behind the dashboard. Fortunately, the car was not derailed, but the deer was a total wreck. Mr. Thoney, incidentally, still remembers his fastest trip down the mountain — a 21-minute flight by gravity car right into the center of Mill Valley, eight and one-fifth miles. There were no passengers, of course, and the trip was made at night when all trains were off the road.

An interesting safety feature of the gravity cars of Mount Tamalpais prevented serious accident in case the cars ran off the rails. Pins were placed under the front beams in such a way that the cars rode the inner guard rails to a safe stop on these pins when derailed, but could not possibly take leave of the level right-of-way. Certainly the gravity cars of the Tamalpais Railroad should live on in the memories of thousands who enjoyed this trip as one of the momentous experiences of their lives. It seems unfortunate that one of these tiny vehicles was not preserved as a monument in Mill Valley or Muir Woods — an example of the ingenuity of those who pioneered in enjoying the natural beauty of this picturesque area. Rusting pieces of a gravity car may be stumbled upon in the brush at the end of the old Muir Woods

The glamorous Tavern of Tamalpais looked like this (above) up to 1923. This unusual view barely shows Motor Car No. 1, under the arch behind train. A forest fire in 1923 left the ruins shown below. The following year a more modest structure was erected, as shown in other views.

Branch, but there is nothing left to show what pleasures this car brought to Californians and visitors of another generation, except their memories.

The operations of the Mt. Tamalpais & Muir Woods Railway went on as calmly and precisely as if it had been on the side of a mountain for centuries. Scheduled trains ran punctually, day after day and year after year; the gravities coasted down the hill without flaw or accident. Yet there was always plenty of excitement under the surface. The train crews remember thrilling experiences; a few of them even made the front pages of San Francisco newspapers. Also, built as it was upon a mountain steeped in Indian story and superstition, by men of imagination in a time of speculation and expansion, it is only natural that legends and stories and even jokes about the Tamalpais Mountain Railroad enjoyed wide circulation.

In an issue of the *San Francisco Call* just before World War I a story appeared about the reigning president of the railroad, C. F. Runyon. One night Runyon attended an elaborate banquet in "The City" and was unable to leave until just enough time to catch the last ferry and train to Mill Valley. There, in the early hours of the morning, he decided, as becomes the president of a railroad, to take one of the rail motor cars and go "up to Muir Woods" to spend the night in one of the cottages there.

"We scared up three deer on the trip up and another coming down this morning," Runyon related. "One of them got caught in a stretch of track so that he had to run ahead of the car for about a hundred yards. For nearly half this distance I reached out and patted him on the back. The more I patted, the faster the deer ran, but it was downgrade and the motor kept up with him until we reached an open space, when the animal shot off into the woods." So the newspaper reported the incident, adding that "Gregory's fish story has been beaten" by this new one about the Tamalpais railcar's race with a deer, with the railroad president acting as jockey for both.

Roy Graves tells about night trains to the summit with special parties, when a veritable gale would be blowing at the top of Tamalpais. With windows rattling madly and wind howling and pushing at the building, the guests would decide on a hasty retreat back to sea level, lest they be blown away during the night. There would be great consternation and bustling about outside by the train crew, banging of tools and curses tossed freely into the gale.

The engine's headlight had to be unbolted and carried inside the building to be lit up out of the wind, then taken back and fastened up on the locomotive again. The headlight was heavy, possibly as much as 150 pounds, and it was a most unpleasant task. Those were great nights, the crew never knowing when the force of a strong wind off the ocean would blow the light wooden coaches right over as the train ran briefly along the very tip of an exposed ridge near Pie Siding, or "Pieville."

Then there were the Tamalpais fires. In the summer of 1913 a tremendous forest fire threatened the Mt. Tamalpais & Muir Woods Railway, the tavern, and several towns in Marin County, including Mill Valley. For five days the fire raged, battled by Army troops from San Francisco Presidio, by foresters, railroad employees and a hastily organized committee of Mill Valley residents. In the first twelve hours, on July 7th, the fire burned over 2000 acres in the Fern Canyon area on the south side of the mountain, then next day swept up the peak toward the tavern. Firemen from as far away as San Francisco were rushed to the scene, turning one arm of the blaze away from Muir Woods just in time.

On the third day the fire burst out of control and headed for Mill Valley, Larkspur and other towns at the eastern base of the mountain. Over 7000 men were now fighting the wind-driven blaze; business in the towns was at a standstill; residents were burying their silver and fleeing toward the waters of the bay. Two San Francisco evening newspapers on July 9th headlined "MILL VALLEY IN FLAMES . . . DOOMED" — much to the later disgust of Marin editors. On the 11th the fire was conquered, leaving the southerly slopes of Tamalpais above the railroad line black in the sun. Not a building, however, had been burned; the railroad was untouched.

But the Mountain Road had played a dramatic part in the heroic work of fire fighting, running a continuous service of special trains carrying firefighters first to West Point, and afterwards to the places on the line nearest the fire. The day after the conflagration started, when the tavern was seriously threatened at the summit, a train was rushed up to evacuate all employees and guests to a place of safety below. Wet blankets were hastily thrown over the heads of women and children, but as the engine cautiously inched its way down through the smoke, these blankets were rapidly dried out by the heat from both sides of the track. One newspaper dramatically reported that cases of champagne in one

SIGHTSEEING IN THE RUINS

Neither snow nor fire halted regular operation of the Mt. Tamalpais & Muir Woods Railway. Here Gravity No. 16 sits amid the ruins of the Summit Tavern, done in by the 1923 fire. Trains kept running; this was an added "sight."

THE THONEY BROTHERS

Volley Thoney (below) in engine No. 8 at the summit, 1920. He was married to the sister of Roy and Cliff Graves and worked on the mountain road until its end in 1930. At right, his brother, Frank Thoney, conductor, stands at the summit ticket booth with T. J. DeLasaux, agent.

—BOTH PHOTOS, A. C. GRAVES-PENNINGTON COLLECTION

of the cars were opened and the wine poured over the coverings when they became unbearably hot. However, this story was vigorously denied by Mrs. Grace Gilliland, wife of the manager of the tavern. She maintained that the champagne was opened only to give "big draughts to the ladies who needed it as a bracer."

Mrs. Gilliland related a thrilling tale of flames seething and darting in the sides of the open summer cars, now catching a flimsy shirtwaist or igniting straw hats or skirts. They had very little water, which had been used in wetting the blankets, hence the necessity for using champagne for parched throats. At times, the trainmen reported, the rescue train was surrounded by flames at least fifty feet in height and roaring like "a blacksmith's forge." The conductor was busy comforting his charges, especially at one part of the journey when it looked as if they would never reach safety. As in the later great fire of 1929, we can picture the worried engineer and fireman, their eyes bloodshot with heat and smoke, guiding their clattering Shay engine through the inferno and concentrating solely upon getting their passengers out of danger.

The railroad emerged from the fire unscathed, except for blistered paint on the sides of a few coaches. Pictures of the fire fighting show the stubby engines right in the thick of battle; they certainly played a big role in keeping damage to a minimum. And, as if to prove to all that no great harm had been done and that Tamalpais was here to stay, the management audaciously advertised a special reduced-rate "Moonlight Excursion" to the Summit Tavern on Saturday, July 19th, with music and dancing, for only a dollar round-trip.

The praises of Tamalpais sung by Robert Louis Stevenson and Gertrude Atherton sent such prominent people as Helen Gould, the "railroad queen," international groups of scientists, visiting nobility and conventionnaires by the thousands sightseeing up the mountain. The railroad company advertised constantly in travel folders all over the world, in scores of newspapers and in San Francisco theatre programs and guides. People were urged to ride the famous "wiggle train" to the Summit of Tamalpais and look down on eighty cities and towns, see twenty of California's counties, view Mount Diablo and Mount St. Helena, and even majestic Shasta on the clearest of days. The gravity trip was advertised as the "longest roller coaster ride in the world."

Small profits were realized in 1913 and 1914 and the mountain road looked forward with eager expectation to the great Fair Year of 1915, while maintaining tracks and equipment at a bare minimum level. The Secretary's Report of October 22, 1914, is a lengthy document full of misery and woe, with details of penny-saving repairs and hopeful anticipation of 1915. Rails, ties, frogs and switches on the main line were in "depreciated condition." Cuts were too narrow and several trees were too close to the track — a danger to passengers using the running boards of cars, he observed.

Equipment was admittedly not up to standards set by the Interstate Commerce Commission. Neither, for that matter, was the method of operation at the approach of 1915. Couplings and hand-holds for trainmen just barely met California safety requirements; there was absolutely no system for handling extra trains, and the Secretary advocated written train orders for non-scheduled trains — as was done on regular railroads. No uniform set of hand signals was in use, either; one man's "Go Ahead" sign was like another's "Back Up," making it advisable for the enginemen to know in advance who was giving the signals in order that correct action could be taken. Even the official "Brass Hats" had a hard time getting along, it would appear. The two company hotels competed against one another, and both joined forces against the railroad part of the organization. Every department was trying to do the other's job and nothing was accomplished efficiently or well. The Secretary regretfully reported that employees used the company phone for their own long-distance calls, smoked on duty and otherwise showed lack of a proper pride in their railroad. About the only matter of agreement among officials and employees of the Tamalpais Railway would seem to have been a hearty contempt for hikers, and the Secretary felt that this attitude was perhaps unwise.

During the 1915 boom the railroad carried an average of 700 passengers daily in the busy summer months, while the San Francisco Exposition was attracting people from all over the United States. Ten new gravity cars were added, at $230 per car; the Muir Woods Branch was extended a half mile to the new inn site. In September Engine No. 3 was sold, after she and the other four Shays — No's. 4, 5, 7 and 8 — had carried and pushed the mountain trains to the end of their most successful season. They had

NUMBER 9 HEISLER

Last locomotive to be purchased for Mt. Tamalpais service was No. 9, a Heisler-type geared engine of 36 tons. Running underneath the engine can be seen the central driving shaft, which was turned by the cylinders, one on either side. The No. 9 was a cluttered-up homely piece of motive power in service, but proved to be an excellent engine. She was the last Tamalpais locomotive in existence when residents of Mill Valley went searching for a monument in 1951.

even operated "doubleheaders" — one engine with five coaches coupled to another with three coaches.

At the very end of 1917 came the first drastic cutback in service. It had been the custom each winter to run only one train daily and three on Sundays — about half the usual summer service. But now the Railroad Commission gave the company permission to suspend all daily runs, except the "Lee Street Local," from November to March of each year. One train to the Summit was operated on Sundays and holidays only, but nothing at all to Muir Woods. In requiring that the local be retained, however, the Commission allowed the fare to be raised from five to ten cents.

Back came the mountain railroad with a bang in the summer of 1918, announcing its famous ten-dollar, two-day, all-inclusive excursions ("See How We Stretch Your TEN" ads, with a great, tall "$10" in heavy, black type). And these excursions did include everything — transportation from San Francisco to the Summit, meals and night accommodations at the Tavern of Tamalpais, gravity ride to Muir Woods in the morning with lunch at Muir Inn and late afternoon return to the city. Some oldtimers allege that the management unofficially provided feminine companionship, if required, through the private arrangements of the girls themselves. The usual publicity features, stunts and advertising hoopla were continued by the company. They even allowed a two-ton White truck to be fitted with flanged railroad wheels and to draw a flatcar of officialdom to the top of the mountain, showing that "the motor vehicle can actually replace the steam engine with very satisfactory results," according to the conclusions reached by *Motor* magazine for December, 1918.

The railroad's popularity actually grew greater for a time, and schemes like these were what imprinted the memory of this grand transportation oddity so firmly in the minds of so many Californians of a generation ago. But still the fear of wintry weather kept passengers away during the rainy months and Sunday-only winter schedules were maintained until the end of 1920, after which date one train daily throughout the year was ordered as a tourist and advertising feature for the San Francisco region.

The year 1920 witnessed changes in the Mill Valley local service, with a few runs eliminated and discontinuance of local stops by through trains going up the mountain. Numerous improvements in the railroad were made that same year, however, with new yard tracks at the Summit Tavern, itself newly renovated, and a short spur track down the old Bolinas stagecoach road at West Point, for outdoor play crowds. The famous Tamalpais Mountain Theatre had been dedicated by William Kent in 1915 (the first play's success in May 1913 started the project); its location is a natural amphitheatre on the western slope of the mountain, in which the annual production is still presented to capacity crowds. On each third Sunday in May the railroad used to carry thousands to West Point, where they dismounted with picnic baskets, bowler hats and high expectations to walk the remaining mile to the Mountain Play site. From the very first play, this Sunday had been the biggest event of the railroad's season; the plays were always excellent, the setting superb. At the same time, tourist travel was improving as a result of Europe being cut off by the War.

The company bought a Fairbanks motor car in the profitable year of 1920, even recalled Engine No. 7 from service with a logging railway — she had been leased out at $17.50 per day. Finally, in December, another new locomotive was ordered. This was Heisler No. 9, the road's last locomotive and its most powerful. The railroad was making money for a time, while the legends of Tamalpais and her "wiggle train" continued to grow, and the third decade of the 20th Century began its mad rush to depression. The dreaded forest fires continued to take their toll — there had been a fire in 1919 which threatened both Muir Woods and Mill Valley. Another in 1923 wiped out the beloved Tavern completely, and a smaller building was constructed on the same foundation. In contrast, January, 1922, brought a snowstorm that required a rescue train to the Summit, with a hastily improvised snowplow fitted to the pilot of one of the Shays.

The same old names keep cropping up in the Tamalpais story — William Kent and his son, Thomas; the renowned and much-photographed engineer, Jake Johnson, who had started with the railroad in '96. Jake received a special honor in recognition of 25 years' service, when the directors voted him full pay during the winter months of 1921, while service was curtailed. Another noted character on the railroad payroll was Superintendent Bill Thomas, still devoting careful hours to his beloved Shay engines, still making improvements that were to be noted and copied in many countries.

Bill Thomas had come to the mountain railroad on loan from the adjoining North Pacific Coast Railroad to help in getting the Tamalpais line underway in 1896. Then, some time after the

—BOTH PHOTOS, A. C. GRAVES-PENNINGTON COLLECTION

LAST DECADE AT THE TAVERN

Management of the Mt. Tamalpais & Muir Woods Ry. watched competition in the form of the automobile and sightseeing bus cut deeper and deeper into their business, encroach even to the very summit itself. Parking space (above) was provided opposite the new (1924) tavern. Travel fell off considerably in the last five years — only one engine, one coach and a few gravities at the summit "station" in 1929 (below).

Tavern of Tamalpais — Then and Now

These two photographs, taken 25 years apart at the same spot, show the change that has come to the Tamalpais scene with the passing of the railroad. In 1926 the last tavern was two years old, still welcomed travelers by the railroad and the trails. The 1951 scene (below) was taken at a time when the highway to Tamalpais was in a deplorable condition and the crowds of visitors had faded as surely as the Crookedest Railroad. (The road has since been repaired.)

—WALLACE SOREL

—BOTH PHOTOS, A. C. GRAVES-PENNINGTON COLLECTION

COMPETITION TAKES OVER IN MUIR WOODS, TOO

1926 in the lovely, sylvan retreat of old Redwood Canyon, now known as Muir Woods. The crooked Tamalpais Railway still sends its gravity cars and funny engines, but most of the visitors seem to have arrived in the Reos and Buicks and Chevrolets and Hudson Super Sixes and in the White-built Gray Line bus. The gentleman is carrying a camera of the period.

N.P.C. became the North Shore in 1902, Thomas went over and joined the scenic railway permanently as master mechanic. One of his first acts was to change all locomotives from wood to oil burners to reduce materially the high fuel costs. It was Britain's *Locomotive* magazine that later gave the best details of another of Thomas's innovations on the M.T.&M.W. This patented "Porcupine" feedwater heater was an ingenious device for heating water before it was injected into the locomotive boiler, by running it through a series of pipes in the smokebox and up around the inside of the smokestack. The hot gases from the fire, on their way out of the engine, heated the water as much as 46 degrees in tests with a three-car train; it was another method of saving fuel and making the equipment more efficient. And this feedwater-heating device, by the way, accounts for the fat smokestacks on the Tamalpais locomotives.

During the early years there were many broken axles on the railroad's locomotives, perhaps caused by excessive twisting on the very sharp curves. Sometimes four or five breaks a year occurred on Engine No. 8 alone. Again it was Bill Thomas who came up with a solution — he had the axles tapered toward the centers, which, it is said, enabled them to twist a little without cracking. After this innovation Engine No. 4 ran for eight years without a broken axle — the road's record. Thomas was loaned on a consulting basis to the Northwestern Pacific and the mighty Pennsylvania Railroad on similar problems, which he helped them solve in the same way.

Track winding alongside the stream at Mill Valley. Scene near King Street and Corte Madera Avenue about 1900.

CHAPTER FOUR

DECLINING YEARS

Competition . . . Adventures with No. 9 . . . Sunshine Guaranteed . . . Last Days on the Mountain . . . Dramatic Exit

The Mt. Tamalpais & Muir Woods Railway made a nice net profit of $43,000 in 1920, followed by a reasonable $30,000 in 1921. The owners were satisfied with its success and they kept up their barrage in advertising outlets of San Francisco and the general area. And they continued to get thousands of dollars worth of free publicity out of such schemes as the grand plan to mount the world's brightest searchlight atop the mountain ("It will draw thousands to Marin.") They got a lot of newspaper space out of deeding a tract of land to the government for the extension of Muir Woods in 1921. And such 1922 headlines as "Jazz Dancing Invades Muir Woods," along with Marin County's handiness to coastwise rum runners, kept the mountain railroad in the public eye for a number of years.

Even the competitive automobile was used to advantage in advertising the trip to Tamalpais by rail. The first road vehicles to "conquer" the mountain traveled up the railroad crossties all the way. Newspapers periodically recorded these events, with photos of the Reo Speed Wagon, a Buick 6, a Dort covered with Army officer "observers," and a small Chevrolet truck. Then, when an Essex became the first auto to reach the Summit without using the railroad line at all, it won columns and columns of publicity for both Essex and Tamalpais. The road's directors even went about figuring ways and means of turning to their advantage competitive sightseeing buses reaching into Muir Woods. They staged a big newspaper feud with the bus lines, barring them from Mr. Kent's private road and finally instituting a bus service of their own.

There was a real abandonment scare at the end of 1923; the directors announced the consideration of removing rails and using the right-of-way for a sightseeing bus and toll road. This report was later denied — after all, they were still making a profit each year. Probably the construction of a toll road from the north side, up the mountain to the Summit, also spiked plans of the railroad management. There are records that report the railroad's plans to operate joint trips in conjunction with sightseeing buses on the scenic Ridgecrest Boulevard from Fairfax on the north, and with other buses into Muir Woods, the journey to be made one way by scenic railway and the other on these fine, new motor buses. At one time, when this same Ridgecrest Boulevard was nearing completion and the railroad people could see the handwriting on the wall, they spoke officially of acquiring ownership of the toll road for operation along with their railroad. But this plan, like so many earlier ones, never progressed beyond the talking stage.

The railroad went on carrying good loads of passengers during the summer months, in addition to an occasional standard freight car of supplies or a flatcar, perhaps, loaded with a steam shovel to clear a slide up on the mountain. Shopmen had to unhook the safety chains on the wheels of freight cars from other railroads in order for them to be able to negotiate the sharp curves. One interesting "freight" operation of the Tamalpais road was the daily hauling of a four-wheel car with an upright water tank, carrying water from Fern Canyon tank to the Tavern. To this supply was added water from the water tanks of the railroad engines, discharged through a hose into a tank in the tavern basement. The outlet valve was placed three inches above the bottom of the engine tank, however, to leave enough water for cooling the wheels on the descent as far as Fern Canyon, where refills were available. The discovery of a spring near the Tavern in 1921 put an end to this delightful and sanitary practice.

In 1923 a profit of $19,584 was earned. However, business was definitely dropping off with the gradual encroachment of auto roads and the swarming hordes of hikers from the scores of clubs. There could be seen groups of hikers clearing trails Sunday after Sunday, going on to build fine bonfires on the beaches beyond. The annual Mountain Play became itself a mecca for hikers of the whole Bay Area, leaving the railroad to haul the aged and crippled, quite literally. The profit dropped in 1924 to $6032.

Fortunately for the Tamalpais mountain railroad, these same years of growing competition saw also great increases in tourists coming to California. The railroad was able to carry on with moderate success, yet eyeing apprehensively the future for its type of operation. Engine No. 9, bought in 1921 for $16,000, was sold to the Siskiyou Lumber Co. in northern California for $9750. This

—VOLLEY THONEY

THE LAST CROOKED MILE

Engine No. 7 after the great fire of 1929 (above), stored on a siding in Mill Valley; she was later repaired and sold for service in the Philippine Islands. The unhappy scene below shows the rails and ties being removed after 34 years; engine No. 8 is working with this slowest and saddest of mountain trains.

—ROY D. GRAVES

36-ton Heisler had enjoyed an interesting three-year life on Tamalpais. Hailed by local papers when it arrived, the "thoroughly modern engine" was explained fully to residents and travelers in columns of newsprint that would have delighted the eye of a veteran railroad enthusiast. It was carefully pointed out that, whereas the four Shays had the driving shaft along the right side and outside the wheels, the Heisler shaft was in the center, beneath the boiler, geared to the extreme front and rear axles. Today's eye, attuned to chrome and streamlining, wonders at such devotion to mechanical detail. But so many writings, guidebook and technical, had been printed on the powerful operation of the odd Tamalpais Shays, that this data on No. 9 was probably quite proper and interesting to the average reader of the early 'Twenties.

The No. 9 was, of course, the road's most powerful engine, and she did gallant work on the days when extra trains were required. On Mountain Play Day it was customary for the 9-Spot to work two round trips to the Summit and two to the Woods, a total of nearly fifty miles with capacity loads, averaging about eight miles per hour. Easter Sunrise Services was another Mt. Tamalpais feature at which Engine No. 9's power was needed. But the locomotive had bad habits that kept her from being a favorite. One former employee tells us that she "wouldn't steam" at first, and the flues would be leaking by the time her train reached Lee Street on the way up. Both injectors would be open at all times, pumping water, and still the engineer would be forced to stop and blow water into the boiler. It wasn't unusual to find the crew using the Tavern's fire hose to keep No. 9's tank full at the Summit.

It must have been a horrifying sight for the fire-fearing residents to see Engine No. 9 wearing a five- or six-inch cap of fire from her stack on trips up the mountain at night, with the smokebox on the front a cherry red upon reaching the top. Because the driving shaft was underneath the boiler, the firebox had to be shallow, creating all this extra fire and heat, even to the extreme of igniting wooden wrecking wedges carried on the sides. A certain startled brakeman received a bad burn while lifting the engine's re-railing frog from beside the boiler one trip. It is reported that after this engine's flues were electrically welded much of the trouble was ended and she thereafter steamed so well that she never "made smoke" on the mountain.

Volley Thoney claims to have been laid off for a time because he approached a speed of sixty miles per hour with No. 9 — one minute flat from Lee St. to the station in town! It is a fact that this engine was the cause of much cracked plaster along Blithedale Avenue in Mill Valley, with her sharp, heavy exhaust a veritable roar of sound. When the shopmen got No. 9 in shape she was a wonderful engine.

There was considerable trouble at first with burning out a bearing on her rear set of wheels — quite often, and at ninety dollars per bearing. Nothing happened when the crew could manage to leave late and run the tail off the engine with no stops — good speed, lots of oil, momentum added up to good performance. But let her run slowly, with stops, and she would heat up the rear truck bearing, and no one could give a reason for it. One day Thoney was running the engine and watched his fireman scooping sand into the firebox to clean soot out of the flues. Some of this sand spilled on the cab deck and was blown down onto the rear truck, right on the bearing. The very next day Thoney fixed a metal plate below the damper to keep this sand out, and the engine thereafter ran like a top. He claims that the Northwestern Pacific's traveling engineer never could figure out why the troubles suddenly ceased, especially after he had been called repeatedly to assist the mountain road's mechanics. Thoney says he manipulated his metal shield to the point that everyone left No. 9 for him to run, as he was the only engineer who could make her behave.

So Engine No. 9 was sold in 1924, eventually to serve out her years as a logging train locomotive for the Dolbeer & Carson Lumber Co., near Eureka, on the northern coast of the state. It was in the same year that the Summit Tavern was rebuilt, on a simpler scale, this time to serve automobile sightseers as well as travelers on its parent railway. The Mt. Tamalpais & Muir Woods was still advertising extensively in the newspapers and guides of the area, using the familiar outline of the mountain and the appropriate symbol of the spinning top with the name of the company inscribed. One series of ads exploited the never-failing sunshine on the mountain, no matter how thick the fog in town. "Fares Refunded if the Sun Fails to Shine" cried the ads; seven round trips a day from Mill Valley to the Summit were scheduled. Special parties were carried at the hint of a request; special days were celebrated with extra trains and events.

Those wonderful New Year's Eve parties at the Tavern! There are hundreds of people in Marin and San Francisco who still tell about them. It is said that even during Prohibition times nothing was lacking at the Tavern. Perhaps the inaccessibility of the mountain top, the good-fellowship of railroad and tavern employees, and the nearness to the rum-running coastline combined to make a rare spot of the top of Tamalpais on New Year's Eve. Eclipses, full moons, Mountain Plays, the New Year and Christmas, Thanksgiving Dinner at the Tavern — all were gay occasions for extra trains and happy throngs on the railroad. What mattered an occasional fire, or a snowstorm, or even a two-week slide blockade? The Tamalpais Railway always pulled through, got itself running again at the earliest opportunity, always advertising more and better attractions in the face of adversity. There was a time in the early 'Twenties when negotiations were started with the idea of selling out to the Northwestern Pacific Railroad, which connected at Mill Valley. In 1923 the mountain line had even been offered to the United States, in conjunction with Muir Woods and a huge National Park comprising all of the Tamalpais region. Nothing came of either of these schemes.

Abandonment talks were initiated in 1925, causing San Francisco newspapers to mourn the imminent death of the world's crookedest railroad. They regretted publicly that the road had never managed to "get conspicuously on the tourist map," although it had been a true delight to those who had made the trip. San Francisco had never given the road a full share of publicity, which it certainly would have received had it operated within the lively orbit of Los Angeles. Twenty-nine-year histories of the line appeared in the press, with memories of old timers and stories of early operations. Credit was given to the railroad for never having killed a single passenger, the death of engineer Chester Thomas in 1900 being the line's only fatality. Two injuries to travelers were the only bad marks in that respect — a passenger had had his leg broken in 1922 and a woman had been seriously hurt in falling from a gravity car en route to Muir Woods in 1924.

Despite the plans to discontinue service, the little railroad wasn't destined to quietly fold up and fade away. The 1925 talks stopped when it was decided that the railroad could not be converted to a toll auto road in time for the following summer season. From this time to 1929, however, business fell off steadily, most of it to automobiles, while the expense of operating and maintaining the line continued to rise. Part of the railroad management had some interest in the competing Ridgecrest Boulevard toll road from the north, and they joined with the others in the opinion that the rail line had either to change to a toll highway itself or to cease operation entirely. The owners reasoned that auto toll roads could be profitable, and their tavern would still be able to serve "autoists" as well as rail sightseers. Their advertising campaign dwindled appreciably these last three or four years, and it appears obvious from the company's records that the officials and directors were just waiting for the opportunity to get out of the railroad business.

It was the big mountain fire of July 2, 1929, that brought the Mt. Tamalpais & Muir Woods Railway most dramatically to the close of its last chapter. That morning Jake Johnson had noticed a haze over the lower part of the mountain on his way up with the regular train. Early in the afternoon, from the Summit, fire could be seen creeping toward the south side and the rail line, and soon clouds of smoke seemed almost to surround the apprehensive watchers above.

The fear of being trapped and unable to get through the fire sent Jake and his crew and 65 passengers hurrying down the line, the Shay at the head end and old Jake Johnson telling his fireman, "The old gal will make it; we'll get through all right." Clouds of gaseous smoke reached for the train as the forest line was gained; then the cars were passing through waves of suffocating heat. Trainmen emptied the water coolers, wetting handkerchiefs and cloths to cover the faces of the women and children. Although the fire was still some distance from the right-of-way, ties were beginning to smolder from the heat as the train hurried downhill. Coach sides were blistered, roofs smoking, and the engineer up ahead was unable to see through the smoke and heat. Jake guided his train blindly and perfectly through the inferno into the cool shade of Corte Madera Canyon and right up to the station in Mill Valley. They say that his hair was singed and that he was virtually unable to see out of his smoke-filled eyes. Not a single passenger, however, was hurt in any way.

Meanwhile, up on the mountain, Vollie Thoney with Engine No. 7 was helping to fight the fire. The engine crew and a group of volunteer fire fighters held off the fire with hoses from the engine until Jake Johnson's passenger train could get safely through. They stayed at the worst spot until water ran low, then

Motor No. 2 at Muir Woods Inn, the end of the branch line.

Party of sightseers on the way to Muir Woods in Motor No. 2, about 1912. Second from the left is Bonner Whitcomb, while the man at the far right is General Manager Ingram. Fog from the nearby Pacific Ocean can be seen creeping over the peaks in an early-afternoon invasion.

hurried up the hill to Mesa tank, at the Bow-Knot, for another tankful, taking the fire fighters with them. Back to the fire; then the dash up to Mesa again for still more water. This time it was obvious that the fire was too far advanced for the engine to venture back, but one of the volunteers was missing despite the crew's vigorous ringing of bell and blowing of whistle to call them all in.

The No. 7 and her crew went down to find the missing man; there he was, right in the thick of the flames and smoke, squirting water at the base of a 300-foot redwood. They took him aboard, but it was too late to make it back to safety. The cab windows had popped out from the heat; rags and cotton waste had been wrapped around all handles in the cab — they were too hot to touch! Small fires on the cab roof itself had been put out four or five times. But now the very crossties underneath their tracks had been charred beyond burning; off went the engine onto the ground, unable to move. As the engineer and fireman and their passenger staggered up the line out of the fire's killing heat, old Bill Thomas appeared, running down the tracks and crying, "You can't leave her there; you'll get fired for deserting your engine!" He was in tears over the loss of one of his beloved Shays. The train crew and fire fighters escaped in a gravity car from the Bow-Knot down the Muir Woods Branch to Mine Ridge bridge, where an auto was commandeered to carry them by a roundabout way to Mill Valley. Deserted Engine No. 7, her cab, footboards and other woodwork burned off, was later shoved onto a siding in town until the tracks were torn up. In 1934 the cab from a dismantled Northwestern Pacific locomotive was fitted on at Tiburon shops and she was shipped to a logging railway in the Philippines.

Carloads of new ties were ordered after the fire, and the line was actually put back in shape, only to be officially abandoned in the summer of 1930. Engine No. 8 was the last to operate, being used on trains which carried the ripped-up rails down off the mountainside. When the last piece of steel had been torn up, engineer Johnson, who had come to work with the first engine 34 years before, ran No. 8 up an incline and onto a flatcar, whistled out a flag, whistled again to call in the imaginary flagman, gave a last long toot — and that was the end of the Mt. Tamalpais & Muir Woods Railway.

Engine No. 4 was scrapped in 1931; No. 5 was sent, with No. 7, to the Philippines. Shay No. 8 was sold in 1931 for switching service at the Shell Oil refinery at Martinez, but condemned by

—BOTH PHOTOS, T. G. WURM

AFTER THE CROOKED RAILROAD VANISHED

Northwestern Pacific interurban depot (above) in 1940, just three days before the last electric train was replaced by the buses shown. Tamalpais track remains partly visible to right; summit of mountain appears at upper left. One of the last electric trains (below) stops at Park Ave. station, en route to Mill Valley on the single-track branch line of the N.W.P.

Famous No. 9, only remaining Tamalpais locomotive, is mounted on a pedestal at Scotia, California. Property of the Pacific Lumber Company, the engine was spared from the scrapper's torch at the last minute and now sits in silent contemplation of past glories on the mountain.

Shay No. 8 after the abandonment of the Tamalpais railroad went into service in the construction of Hoover Dam. Here she is with a train of loaded aggregate cars at the gravel plant yards, near Boulder City, Nevada, May 4, 1932.

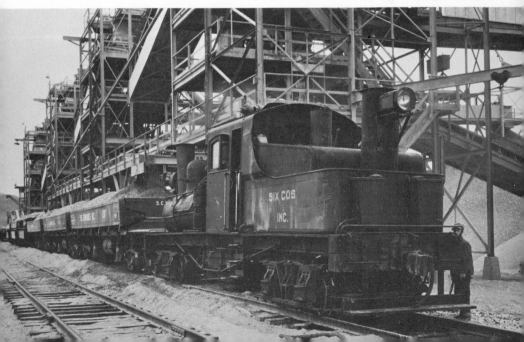

a government inspector and taken back to the shops at Tiburon for an overhaul. Then the 8-Spot went forth again, this time to help switching at the gravel plant at the construction of Hoover Dam. A cut of gravel cars broke loose one day, met No. 8 suddenly; she had to be scrapped. The well-known open passenger cars and beloved gravities were taken apart on the spot, thus erasing the last of the mountain railroad's equipment from the scene.

For many years various sheds and other structures stood at the mouth of the canyon in Mill Valley; these and the station platforms at Mesa and a few water tanks along the line were landmarks to hikers using the roadbed for easy climbing. Today the entire route is intact from the upper end of Corte Madera Canyon to the Summit, used as an emergency fire trail. A Sunday walk up this trail stirs the memory with visions of puffing Shays and gliding gravities, and the glorious views bear out the truth of all stories written about the wonders of the Tamalpais scenic railway.

After abandonment the railroad tracks and equipment passed into the hands of a San Francisco dealer, Fred Botsford, for $15,000. Rails were readily disposed of to logging railways and the ties that weren't serviceable went to work holding up many a Marin County fence and cheering the fireside of many a Marin home. Some car seats found their way into Mill Valley gardens, a lasting reminder to old timers.

The cheerful call of the whistle and the echoing sound of the bell as a mountain train labored through Blythedale and up the hill had vanished. They had been for 34 years an assurance to the people of the valley that all was well with the nearby world. Over the span of a third of a century presidents came and went, a great city was reduced to ashes, a world war was fought — in a rapidly changing world, the railroad was one thing that remained untouched, a souvenir, if you will, from an old order of things that to local people contributed much to the stability of life. As the San Francisco *Chronicle* sadly noted in its farewell editorial, "Progress has its way and commands its price."

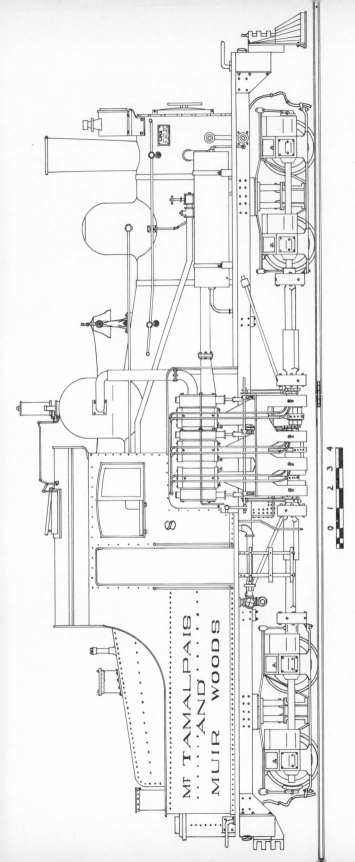

SHAY LOCOMOTIVE NUMBER 8 — Drawn to Scale by C. A. Graves

All Shay-type geared locomotives except some of the earliest models had three cylinders arranged vertically, giving a uniform turning movement to the longitudinal shaft and operating all the wheels by bevel gearing. The shaft was provided with universal joints, giving ample flexibility on the sharpest curves, and, as the entire weight was carried on driving wheels, all were available for adhesion, while the rigid wheelbase was kept very short. A few Shays still operate on logging railways in California and other western states.

Engine	Type	Cylinders	Dimensions Wheels	Weight	Builder	Year	No.	Notes
498	Shay	9x8	26½	40,000	Lima	1893	498	(1)
1	Shay	8½x12	28		Lima	1900	597	(2)
2	Heisler	15x12	36	60,000	Stearns	1896	1005	(3)
3	Heisler			60,000	Stearns	1898		(4)
3	Shay	10x10	28	46,000	Lima	1901	646	(5)
4	Shay	10x10	28	46,000	Lima	1903	832	(6)
5	Shay	10x10	28		Lima	1906	1666	(7)
6	0-4-0 tank	10x16	30	36,000	Porter	1906	3483	(8)
7	Shay	10x10	28	74,000	Lima	1908	1945	(9)
8	Shay	10x10	28½	74,000	Lima	1912	2505	(10)
9	Heisler	13x12	33	72,000	Heisler	1920	1446	(11)

(1) Engine No. 498 was displayed at 1893 Columbian Exposition, Chicago. Came to Tamalpais from Usal Redwood Co. and Dollar Lumber Co. Sold 1904 to Terno Lumber Co., Terno, Wash. Later resold to Coal Creek Logging Co. (1920) and to Lacamas Logging Co., both at Chehalis, Wash. From there it passed through the hands of Zimmerman-Wells-Brown, Portland, Ore., and ended up at the Marcilla Lumber Co., Chehalis, Wash.

(2) No. 1 sold 1904 to Campbell Lumber Co., Campbell, Wash. Then it went to Leona Mill & Lumber Co. and to R. A. Beebe Lumber Co., both at Leona, Wash.

(3) "Joseph G. Eastland"

(4) First No. 3 was named "S. B. Cushing." Found to be unsatisfactory "in cab arrangement," it was returned to the builder in April, 1898.

(5) "Tamalpais," second No. 3, was sold Sept., 1915, to California & Oregon Power Co., Hornbrook, Calif. From there it went to Flora Logging Co., Carlton, Ore., and to Union Lumber Co., Fort Bragg, Calif. Scrapped October 10, 1929.

(6) Scrapped 1931.

(7) No. 5 was rebuilt in 1920 by Pacific Car & Equipment Co., San Francisco. It was sold Nov., 1930, to United Commercial Co., San Francisco, then to Kewanee Boiler Corp., Portland, Ore., after Six Companies, Inc. (Hoover Dam), had rejected it. Went in May, 1937, to Pt. Lamon Lumber Co., Pt. Lamon, P. I.; in May, 1938, to Madrigal Lumber Co. at Pt. Lamon. Was known to be still in service in 1946.

(8) No. 6 had 150 lbs. boiler pressure, exerted 6800 lbs. tractive effort. It was sold in 1915 for $1400. Eventually became No. 2 of Guy F. Atkinson Construction Co.; was stored many years in East Oakland. Scrapped 1944.

(9) To Philippine Islands.

(10) No. 8 was sold through United Commercial Co., to Six Companies for construction work on Hoover Dam. Destroyed in collision with runaway gravel cars.

(11) No. 9 had a boiler pressure of 190 lbs., exerted a tractive effort of 21,500 lbs. It was sold in 1924 for $9750 to Siskiyou Lumber Co., Macdoel, Calif. From there it went to Dolbeer & Carson Lbr., at Falk, near Eureka, Calif. Retired 1951. Permanently displayed at Scotia, Calif.

MOTOR CARS

"Booster" Steam, 4-wheel, with upright boiler.
No. 1 6-passenger. Purchased 1905; retired 1914. Gasoline. Called "Black Maria."
No. 2 25-passenger. Stoddard-Dayton with homemade body. 1909.
No. 3 20-passenger. Kissel Kar, 8-wheel. 1916.
Continental Motor put in, 1922; third motor, 1925.
No. 4 Fairbanks.

ROLLING STOCK

23 passenger coaches: 19 open, with canopy top; 2 half-enclosed; 2 entirely enclosed.

2 flatcars

32 gravity cars: 30-passenger, 4-wheel. Ten steel cars built in company shop; ten purchased in 1915 for $230 each; last 6, in 1920 from Pacific Car & Equipment Co.

For additional information on Engine No. 7 see text; it had a colorful career, even after it left the service of the Mt. Tamalpais & Muir Woods Railway.

There is mention in the company's Minutes of a Shay locomotive being purchased in April, 1903, being rejected and returned to Lima Locomotive Works. No additional information on this engine is available. Mention is also made in the Minutes of an engine being sold to the Hetch Hetchy Railroad, California, in December, 1916. The No. 7 was known to operate in the region served by the Hetch Hetchy, although

1920 records state it was recalled from "lease" to serve again on the mountain road.

An attempt was made by interested residents of Mill Valley in 1952 to have Engine No. 9 returned to the town as a permanent monument to the mountain railroad. Although several people expressed interest, public apathy was such that the plan was abandoned and the engine was enshrined at Scotia, near Eureka.

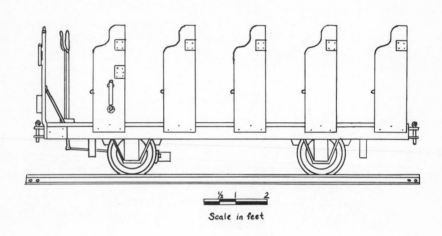

½ 1 2
Scale in feet

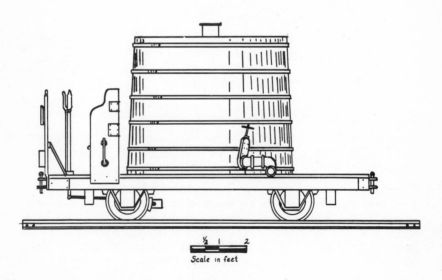

½ 1 2
Scale in feet

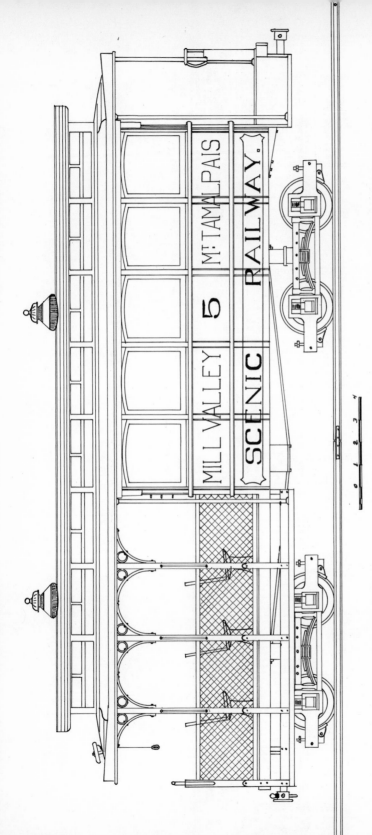

Scale Drawing of the First Tamalpais Passenger Coach. C. A. Graves.

The No. 5 came second-hand from the 42-inch gauge Omnibus Cable Railroad in San Francisco, was placed on standard-gauge trucks and put in Tamalpais service with its original green paint unchanged.

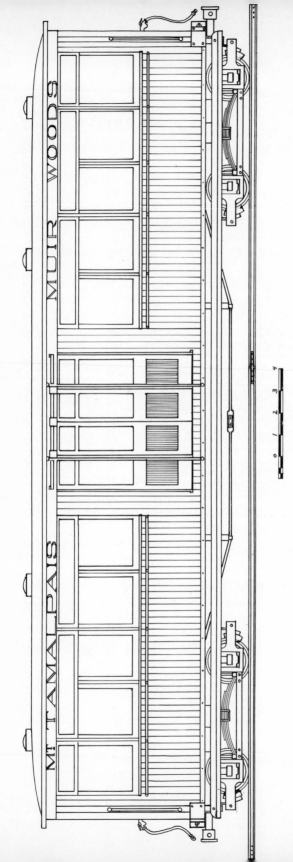

Closed Passenger Coach – Drawn to Scale by C. A. Graves

BIBLIOGRAPHY

Bingham, Helen, *In Tamal Land*. San Francisco: Calkins Publishing House, 1906.

Biographical Directory of the American Congress, 1774-1949. Washington D. C.: Government Printing Office, 1950.

Dickinson, A. B. *Old Railroads, Boats and Redwoods, a Saga of the North Pacific Coast Railroad*. Published serially. Placerville, California: *The Pony Express*, 1952-1953.

Gudde, Erwin G. *California Place Names*. Berkeley: University of California Press, 1949.

Millard, Bailey. *History of San Francisco Bay Region*. Chicago-San Francisco-New York: The American Historical Society, Inc., 1924.

Official Guide of the Railways of the United States, Puerto Rico, Canada, Mexico and Cuba. New York: National Railway Publication Co. (Monthly), various issues, 1896-1930.

Pocket List of Railroad Officials. New York: Railway Equipment & Publishing Co. (Quarterly), various, 1910-1930.

Poors Manual of Railroads of the United States. New York: Poor's Railroad Manual Co. (Annual), 1896-1925.

Railway Equipment Register. New York: Railway Equipment & Publishing Co. (Quarterly), various, 1915-1930.

Road of a Thousand Wonders, The. San Francisco: Passenger Department, Southern Pacific Co., 1908, 45-7.

San Francisco and Oakland, a Visitor's Guide. Rand McNally guide to San Francisco, Oakland, Berkeley, and environs of the bay cities . . . New York, San Francisco (etc.); Rand McNally & Co., various, 1910-1927.

Shaw, Frederic, *Oil Lamps and Iron Ponies*. By Frederic Shaw, Clement Fisher, Jr., and George H. Harlan, Jr. San Francisco: Bay Books, Ltd., 1949.

Talbot, Fred A. *The Crookedest Railway in the World*. Illus. article in *Railways of the World*. London: Cassell & Co., Ltd. (1924); I; 65-71.

United States Works Progress Administration Records Surveys No. 22. *Marin County History*. San Francisco: Historical Records Survey, 1937.

Wagner, H. Howe, *Mount Tamalpais State Park*. United States Works Progress Administration Official Project 665-08-3-147. Sacramento: California State Printing Office, 1941.

Wells, Harry L. *California Names*. Los Angeles: Kellaway-Ide-Jones Co., 1934.

Bibliography *continued* —

PERIODICALS

Brooks, B. "Land of Tamalpais," *Scribner's Magazine* (NY), 38 (July, 1905), 70-9.

Demorest, Richard. "Marin County— Land Beyond the Golden Gate," *This World* Section, San Francisco *Chronicle*, September 23, 1951.

"Electric Mountain Railroads; Mt. Lowe Railway, California," *Scientific American* (NY), 70 (February 3, 1894), 73.

Fraser, James W. "A Crooked Trail Through Hell," *Railroad Stories* (NY), June 1932, 320-5.

French, H. "Wild Places on Tamalpais," *Overland Monthly* (San Francisco), October, 1904.

"Geared Locomotives of the Mount Tamalpais Railway, California," *Scientific American* (NY), 79 (July 16, 1898), 39.

"Last Mt RR Engine Headed for Scrap," *In Between Times* (Pub. by *Mill Valley Record*), October 27, 1951.

"Lighted Cigarette and a Redwood Forest," *Outlook* (NY), 104 (August 2, 1913), 730.

Marsden, M. "Mount Tamalpais," *Popular Science* (NY), May, 1900.

"Mount Tamalpais & Muir Woods Railway, California," *The Locomotive* (London), XXII (July 15, 1916), 145-7.

"Mountain Play of California," *Independent* (NY) 79 (July 20, 1914) 101.

"New Mountain Locomotive," *Scientific American Supplement* (NY), 64 (August 3, 1907), 73-4.

Perry, L. R. "3000 Men Fight Mountain Fire," *Technical World* (Chicago), 20 (January, 1914), 740-2.

"Scaling Mountain Peaks by Elevator," *Scientific American* (NY), 75 (March 15, 1913), 164-5.

Seivers, Walt. "Mt. Tamalpais & Muir Woods Railroad," *Western Railroader* (San Mateo, Calif.), April, 1940; reprinted in issue of March, 1951.

West, J. Seymour, "World's Crookedest Railroad," *Arrowhead*, June, 1909.

Bibliography *continued* —

MISCELLANEOUS

"Marin Magazine," *Independent-Journal* (San Rafael, Calif.), Golden Jubilee Issue (August 19, 1950).

"*Mill Valley & Mt. Tamalpais Scenic Railway, the 'Crookedest Railroad in the World*," (folder); San Francisco: M.V.&M.T.S.Ry., no date.

Mill Valley & Mt. Tamalpais Scenic, Mt. Tamalpais & Muir Woods Railways. Company scrapbooks containing newspaper clippings referring to the railroad company. 1896-1930.

"Mount Tamalpais and Eight Other Sightseeing Trips in and about San Francisco." Pamphlet. San Francisco: "Balloon Route" Excursion Co., (1910).

North American Press Assn. "Standard Guide to San Francisco," 1913.

Records. Lima Locomotive Works, Lima, Ohio.

Records. Mill Valley & Mt. Tamalpais Scenic, Mt. Tamalpais & Muir Woods Railways. Minutes of directors' meetings.

Records. Northwestern Pacific Railroad Company and predecessor companies.

Records. H. K. Porter Co., Pittsburgh, Pa.

Records. Stearns Mfg. Co., Heisler Locomotive Works, Erie, Pa.

Reports. California Railroad Commission.

Files of the *Eastland Press,* Mill Valley, California.

Files of the *Herald,* Sausalito, California

Files of the *Independent,* San Rafael, California.

Files of the *Independent-Journal,* San Rafael, California.

Files of the *Marin Journal,* San Rafael, California.

Files of the *Marin Press,* Sausalito, California.

Files of the *Mill Valley Record,* Mill Valley, California.

Files of the *News,* Sausalito, California

Files of the *Newsletter,* San Francisco, California

Files of the *San Francisco Bulletin.*

Files of the *San Francisco Call.*

Files of the *San Francisco Chronicle.*

Files of the *San Francisco Examiner.*

Files of the *San Francisco News.*

Files of the *Tocsin,* San Rafael, California.

Files of the *Town Talk,* San Francisco, California

INDEX

(Asterisk indicates illustration)